WHY WE DO IT

WHY
WE DO IT

BY
EDWIN DANIEL WOLFF

Essay Index Reprint Series

BOOKS FOR LIBRARIES PRESS
FREEPORT, NEW YORK

First Published 1929
Reprinted 1968

LIBRARY OF CONGRESS CATALOG CARD NUMBER:

68-16990

PRINTED IN THE UNITED STATES OF AMERICA

Dedication

Away back in the olden days, before the time of Moses, a weary writer finished his book. Long and difficult had been the writing of it—a brush of frayed reed-end tracing hieroglyphs laboriously on sheet after sheet of papyrus. The author read it over again, in its final beautified script. It was soul-satisfying.

"And now to gain favor for it," he smiled, and wrote another sheet which he placed at the very beginning. On this new sheet he wrote, "I dedicate this book to His Eternal Lordship, The Pharaoh of Egypt." That was a slick idea. The Eternal Lordship would be flattered pink at the honor; he would recommend the book to his courtiers; additional copies might be ordered. That long-dead, unknown and now mythical author was the papa of all the advertising men.

For centuries after that first dedication, books and plays continued to enlist the support of the rich and powerful in just that way. Then, within the past 150 years or so, with the spread of education, readers began buying books in quantities. The dedication became needless for business purposes; it remained as a courtesy.

So the smart thing for me to do would be to dedicate this volume to my publishers to encourage them to push its sale. But it is my first non-technical book. I have a wife. I have to live with my wife; I don't have to live with the publishers. Therefore—

THIS BOOK
IS DEDICATED TO
MY WIFE

Why Authors Write Acknowledgments

The average author needs help. You'd know that from reading his book, of course. But in gathering his material and in verifying his facts he has to call on others. He'd like to pay them, if he had the money. Lacking that—and because some people will do out of kindness what they wouldn't do for a fee—he gives those who aided him a little free advertising.

Maybe I will be pardoned, then, if I express keen appreciation to Miss Dorothy Woodworth for collecting many of the facts which are set out on the following pages. Miss Inez Dunlap secured for me some rare information without which this present volume would have been incomplete. Especially am I indebted to Miss Carmelita E. O'Neill, who, in addition to suggesting a number of valuable criticisms, typed the entire manuscript. Mr. Frederick A. Hughes, Dr. Saxe E. Commins and Mr. Loyd Ring Coleman supplied thoroughly welcome encouragement while I wrestled with the first draft over my Corona. Mr. Sidney Crossett drew the illustration of the hat.

I forget who made the paper on which the pages were typed, but it cost me $4.50.

FOREWORD

This is a marvelously strange world into which we are born.

To the newly-arrived baby it offers an unceasing array of established customs and habits. All of these require explaining, and childhood may be described as the age of "Why?" Endlessly the child asks the reason for things as they are. "Why is the sky blue?" "Why is sugar sweet?" "Why mustn't I?" Fortunately, most of these questions can be answered, but occasionally even the keenest intellect is at a loss to reply adequately, as when the little boy asked his father, "Why isn't a cat a dog?" Evolutionist and Fundamentalist can both answer that to their own satisfaction, but any explanation vouchsafed to a child will evoke further cross-examination.

During childhood there are so many things demanding a share of our attention—we must eat, and play, and sleep, and explore, and experiment, and fight. Few are the hours in a day and many are the things to be learned. We absorb what we can; wearily we let the rest go. All too soon come adulthood and the struggle for self-support. No longer is there time to ask, "Why?" Far more likely is it that we have youngsters of our

9

Foreword

own, who occupy our spare time with answering and evading their infinite whys.

So this remains an interesting old World. We may poke an inquiring Jack Horner thumb into it almost at random and pull out a dozen plums of startling fact. It is the purpose of this book to bring a few of those truth-plums out on the table where we may all see them and have a taste. But we shall not bother with authorities, and bibliography, and footnotes.

Do you have the same trouble with footnotes that I do? It exasperates me beyond all patience to find myself in the middle of a deeply absorbing sentence and then come across an interruption in the shape of a number or an asterisk that directs my attention to the lower margin of the page, only to find there some inconsequential reference that I don't care a hoot about seeing. Something like this, "The protective development of the horny epithelia, universally present in the mammalia and to an almost equally unlimited extent in the entire vertebrate kingdom * . . . *Footnote:* * Proc. Psych. Soc., XII, 468-O, 1924; *vide* also Kugeleisen, Unt. d. An., Ed. 1899, pp. 63-64; Jiggs and D. Moore, Res. So. Am. Edent., p. 1008, note; Zwischenmuschelschahlen, Schweinerei der Spitzbubensgesellschaft, orig. ed., Append. M, p. 897, note." That sort of thing drives me nuts. And when I firmly resolve to skip these indices (and afterwards steal a surreptitious glance at the footnotes while turning the page) as often as not I discover some juicy bit that I wouldn't have missed for the world; like, "The same was said to be true of Martha Custis on the eve of her marriage to George Washington, though this is indignantly denied by friends of the family."

There isn't any of that in this book. Everything that the average reader could reasonably expect for his $2.50 is printed in its proper place within the text.

One thing, though, I must make very clear. This volume is written for entertainment as well as instruction. Many of the subjects treated are open to long and sometimes endless controversy. Wherever I could find a majority of authorities in favor of any one explanation for a present custom I have given that reason, purposely ignoring others—perhaps just as valid—to avoid dry and seemingly interminable discussion. Where authorities were evenly divided I have chosen the historical explanation which appeared to me more logical or more interesting.

ED WOLFF

CONTENTS

13

Contents

WHY WE DO IT

WHY WE CAST RICE AT BRIDES

REALLY, if we wanted to observe the spirit of the Eighteenth Amendment and the Volstead Law strictly, we should find some other name for our newly married damsels. For, according to the derivation of the word, we would be quite justified in asking of a young husband, "Well, Charley, how's your brewer?"

Bride means just that—brewer. Why, even the wedding feast was known to our Anglo-Saxon ancestors as the "bride-ale"; and—with a slight change of pronunciation—we still employ the term; we have a "bride-ale" party and a "bride-ale" ceremony, though in spelling it we drop the final e and write "bridal." Occasionally, before the ceremony, the groom is deftly filled with the idea that in his new-formed family it is going to be spelled bridle—but it never is. King that he was, he steps down off his throne with the cutting of the bridal cake.

That cake itself has a rather involved history. Among the old Romans there existed a form of near-marriage, of which the essential feature in the ceremony was the eating, by bride and groom, of a special kind of cake; and the lady held in her hand three ears of wheat. After a while the cake fell into disuse as a part of the ritual, but even into the Middle Ages the bride continued to hold in her hand or to wear somewhere about her person the traditional wheat-ears.

You know girls—they couldn't miss a wedding. Back in those days, just as now, they would cluster around the church-door to see the bride come out. And they took to tossing grains of wheat at the bride and then scrambling for them, probably to put them under the pillow at night and dream of their own future husbands. Later the wheat was cooked into a dry sort of cake which was broken over the bride's head, though it does seem to us that this performance might have been left for the groom to attend to after his wife's first batch of baking was set before him. But it was the cake idea come back again, you see.

Then Elizabeth became Queen of England and the custom changed again; now every guest received a small "bride-ale" throwing cake, and the instant that the bride crossed the threshold the entire collection was showered upon her. Those cakes which lighted on her head or shoulders were most prized by the scrambling attendants. Once more a change took place; these little cakes merged into one huge affair, elaborate and symbolically decorated—the forerunner of our own wedding cakes.

When wheat-throwing ceased because the grains were baked into cakes the onlookers at a marriage felt a sense of deprivation; they were accustomed to hurling things at the bride and they wanted to continue that pleasant practice. True, the guests were supplied with wheat-cakes to toss, but the uninvited audience wasn't. So these latter were put to it to find something that would take the place of the "old-fashioned" wheat; and because rice symbolized fertility, and was near enough like wheat to satisfy the requirements, besides being white and clean and cheap, they chose rice. To this day we cast rice at a bride, though not one of us in twenty associates it with the idea of fertility. We do it just because it has always been done, we think. Hereafter we shall know why, and with the rice offer a prayer.

Somebody is wondering why we throw old shoes. Good thought. In days of old before knights were bold, or even dreamed of, men literally took their brides. A young warrior decided that he could no longer live happily without a certain flapper; it happens yet, for that matter. That old-timer, not being able to gain the parental consent, staged a raid. He and his closest friend sneaked up on the girl—who probably put herself in danger of being kidnapped on purpose—the lover grabbed her and away they went. If irate father or brothers followed, the friend fought them off while the blissful couple made their escape. Do you see where the "best man" originated?

In such a conflict spears were hurled, and clubs, and stones. Every now and then, of course, dad would give

19

his consent without argument. But it hardly flattered the daughter's vanity to be captured thus easily. Nor was it any testimony to the young buck's prowess that he merely walked off with the maiden. So they staged fake battles; papa lobbed a light stick or two ever so gently in their direction, pretending to be terribly angry, and the couple made believe to be scurrying away—just as our newly-weds sneak off from their assembled guests now, though goodness knows nobody is going to stop them. Therefore we today must throw things, too.

But why shoes? Well, away back in the old days in Palestine the Israelites, instead of signing a contract and attaching a seal, as we do, used to take off a shoe before witnesses when closing a deal. There is an interesting incident of this kind in the Book of Ruth; and in Psalm lx we read, "Over Edom will I cast out my shoe," signifying the relinquishment of ownership and protection. So, too, when a man gave up his daughter to her suitor he removed his shoe, thus legally putting her into the possession of the other man. In time those two customs became entangled; we had to cast something and we had to remove a shoe. So we simplified matters—some hundreds of years ago, of course—by combining the two. And now we throw shoes—old ones, for economy's sake and because our ancient forefathers, in casting a shoe, used one that they had worn.

A paragraph or two back we read that men once

literally stole their wives, fighting off enraged kinsmen. Where did they go with their lovely captives? Into hiding for a few weeks until the storm blew over and they could bring the lady back into the tribe without inciting a riot, or so that her father, belonging to another tribe, might not recapture her. Time was reckoned by changes of the moon and this was the sweetest moon of all—a real moon of honey. Nowadays the couple pretends to be fleeing—though everyone helps them get away—and off they go on a honeymoon.

Well, well, well! It's a great old world, isn't it?

WHY WE CALL HIM MISTER

WHILE I was standing on Market Street in Chattanooga one winter day waiting to keep an appointment, I idled away the time by watching an old colored man seated on a stool vending roasted chestnuts. Down the street came a white-haired gentleman, and as he passed the darky greeted him in friendly fashion, "Hoddy, Jedge, hoddy; how is yo' Honah dis mawnin', Jedge? Yassuh." Then, seeing me regarding him with a smile, the darky grinned back and tempted me craftily, "Mister, buy some fresh roasted chistnuts? Dey's sho' fine; on'y tin cints, mister."

I bought, of course. No Southerner can resist the blandishments of a negro who understands the type. To make conversation I queried, "Been in this country long, uncle? Maybe you were here and saw the Battle of Missionary Ridge." To which he replied, "Sho'ly. Bawn right hyah, boss. Befo' de war I used to belong to de Tuckersons. Ol' Cap'n Jim Tuckerson was mah master. Yassuh!"

The old darky, within a few minutes, had addressed me as "Boss," and "Mister." He had greeted another gentleman as "Judge." And he had spoken of old Captain Jim as his former "Master." In all four cases he had supplied identical titles, yet he did not realize it.

Among the ancient Romans a judge was known as a "magister." From this word is descended almost unchanged the name by which many of our own judges are known—magistrate. The head of our Supreme Court is the Chief Magistrate; in other words, the principal judge.

But not all of our Latin-born words come to us directly. Sometimes they filter through other languages before they reach ours. That has happened in this case. Latin *magister* becomes Old French *maistre;* at present its French form is *maître.* A distinguished lawyer in France today bears the honorary title *Maître.* But a manager is also a *maître*—we have potatoes on the bill-of-fare cooked in the style of the *maître d'hôtel.*

In Spanish, another tongue through which some Latin has been inherited by English, the word took an almost identical form—*maestro.* In mentioning an instructor in a school the English speak of the master; the principal is the headmaster. In Madrid, in Monterey and in Rio de Janeiro, where Spanish is spoken, the teacher is termed a *maestro.* Thus, trickling down to us through the ages, the Latin title for a judge has come to mean a master as well.

French has a habit of inserting itself into other languages. Consider one of the newer important and widely used inventions—the automobile. Its frame is a *chassis,* the rear part is a *tonneau*, its driver is a *chauffeur*—all French expressions. During an earlier age, when French was the universal language of diplomacy and a necessary part of the education of all cultured Englishmen, the borrowings were even more frequent. So when Lord Bazookus returned to London after a visit to Paris he would remember that the French gentlemen called each other Maistre Le Tournat and Maistre de Roussy, and he found it not strange to hear Englishmen soon addressing their friends as Maistre Smith and Maistre Jones. *Maistre* soon became anglicized to Mister; and to this day you and I are Mister to those who would pay us due respect without intimacy.

We remember, though, that when we were thirteen years old we were not misters. On the rare occasions when somebody mailed us a written invitation to a party or a lacy heart-shaped Valentine—oh, happy days!—our name was prefixed with Master. This word has the same ancestry, of course; but in English households the sons are still spoken of by the servants as the "young masters," and nowadays our growing boys have to pass through the stage of being masters before they arrive at the proud distinction of being fully adult misters. Aren't folks silly?

After a master grows into a mister he commonly takes unto himself a wife. She becomes the feminine head of his household. He is the mister, she is the misteress, just as the English used to call a tailor a seamster and his sister-worker a seamsteress, or the son of a king a prince and his sister a princess. The spelling has been shortened to mistress, but the sense remains unchanged.

In just the same way as a man and his young son had both been *maistres,* so married and single ladies up to within thirty years of our Revolutionary War had both borne the honorary title Mistress. About that time—there have always been purists—some finicky people began to think there ought to be a distinction. Maybe the ladies who had captured a husband believed that those not so fortunate ought to be reminded of it, though far be it from me to bring up such an imputation. Anyway, Mistress when it meant a bachelor female became abbreviated to Mis. and when it meant a wife was currently contracted to Mrs. And so a mother is now a Mrs. and her daughter is a Miss. Yet both are the feminine form of master, as any man instinctively knows who has to live with either or both.

WHY WE ASK "WHY"

SOME years ago, on a visit to the Zoölogical Garden at San Pedro Springs Park, in San Antonio, I was much struck by the actions of a small monkey confined by himself. Three sides of his cage were of iron bars so far apart that he could gaze through them at what was going on around him. The fourth side was built up solidly of wooden boards, in one of which was a knot-hole. For the better part of an hour, as I watched him, the monkey spent most of his time with his eye to the knot-hole, though there was nothing more of interest occurring on that side than elsewhere. From time to time he would apparently rest satisfied that the scene hidden by the boards concealed nothing of importance, or other matters claimed his attention, and he would lark about on his swing or distract himself with a wooden ball. But invariably after a few moments he would be overcome by his insatiable curiosity and back he would leap to the knot-hole, where—resting his hands on his knees ludicrously as a man would under similar circumstances—he peered out eagerly, seeking to penetrate the mystery of the unknown.

Everywhere about us we see signs of that same desire. As I write, a mother-robin outside my window is nervously intent on teaching two young fledgelings to fly. Obedient to their instinct, they watch carefully as she flutters her wings and hops enticingly from twig to twig. Once in a while, encouraged by her chirrups and extravagant anxiety, they flicker their own little wings and essay a breathless flight of twelve inches. Enthralled at their daring, the mother bird carols a vibrant chittering of praise and laudation; she "nize babies" them for all the world to hear. And then, while she turns her back to tempt them farther with a more venturesome hop, the two youngsters divert their attention from her and take appraising pecks at a waving leaf, ogle something snuggling in a crevice of the tree-bark, eye in astonishment the moving of their own shadows—exploring, testing, experimenting, seeking on their own part to penetrate the mystery of the unknown.

Every boy who was raised on a farm knows that young chicks manifest curiosity for a far shorter time than do calves; and a pup discovers so many marvels to claim his avid interest that it wracks one's patience often to train him. The higher we go in the scale of mental power the more obvious and enduring is the craving of the young for acquaintance with their surroundings. Indeed, if we wished to classify roughly the mature intelligence of several animals hitherto unknown we might do it quite accurately by observing how long and how earnestly their young interested them-

27

selves in trying to penetrate the mystery of the un-known.

Now, while man is unquestionably and immeasurably superior to all animals, yet he shares one thing in common with them—his young come into the world untaught. The millions upon millions of marvels which await the denizens of this planet must be learned by our children; and if proof were wanting that mankind exceeds all other forms of life in brain-power it would be found in the fact that the curiosity of children can never be satisfied. They want to know, they want to know, they want to know—eternally they din into our ears the formidable question, "Why—why—why?" Happy the parent whose child never tires of asking why. That is a most comforting sign—the continuing growth of a healthy mentality.

The most intelligent of our great men, it would seem, never outgrow the why habit. Edison's many inventions sprang from his habit of ever confronting Nature with "Why?" As results of some of his whys we have such conveniences and necessities as electric lamps, phonographs, moving pictures. Roentgen demanded of Nature why his unexposed photographic plates became fogged—and discovered the X-ray. The Wright brothers insisted that Nature tell why a plane couldn't fly while a bird could—and learned the secret of mechanical flight. Eastman wanted to know why flexible celluloid strips wouldn't take the place of glass plates

28

Why We Ask "Why"

for holding sensitized film—and on the answer he built Kodak, the country's largest consumer of pure silver bullion (except the government mint) using in its own business the equivalent of one-eleventh of all the silver mined in the United States. Ford wanted to know why an automobile couldn't be built at a low price—and became the world's first billionaire.

Yes, if nothing else distinguished man from the brutes he would still be set apart from all the remainder of creation by his constant and ever-hungry habit of asking why. Human intelligence is never satisfied. Forever it strives to penetrate the mystery of the unknown. This is man's great non-spiritual distinction.

And this intense mental craving brings its own reward. For there is a delight in acquiring knowledge, in learning facts that have been hidden from us. More, it is an ever-expanding joy, because every new truth added to our former store raises another why. Information has been compared to a fire in the night—as fast as the circle of light enlarges it increases the circle of surrounding darkness. Each advance in human knowledge is but an explanation of what had hitherto been unexplained. And each explanation inevitably raises the further question, "What is the explanation of that explanation?" Thus we say to the electrician, "You tell me that my electric bulb gives light because the wire filament resists the current and therefore glows—but why does the filament resist the current? And why does

29

resistance cause a glow? And if the filament resists, why does the current flow at all?"

So we ask why, because we are human beings and feel within us that we are capable of utilizing whatever we can understand. Ours is the glory of having built civilization, ours the task to build it ever higher. Powerful machines we can make to substitute for our puny muscles; delicate mechanisms like the germ-slicers of anatomists replace our clumsy hands, the microscope and telescope for their purposes enormously excel the human eye; with the radiometer we measure the heat of distant stars; with the spectroscope we learn of what gases and metals the stars consist; the microphone turns into thunder the tread of a fly which is inaudible to our ears. All our natural organs for coping with the world about us can be replaced to our advantage by man-made devices—all except the human brain. That is the most wonderful piece of equipment that we know. Nothing that we have can take its place, except a better one.

And man is constantly striving to make his brain better. He wants to know. From the moment when his infantile intelligence first begins to dawn until his eyes close in the last long sleep his brain is always challenging the universe with the question of all questions —"Why—why—why?"

WHY WE OBSERVE SUNDAY

REMEMBER the Sabbath to keep it holy. Six days shalt thou labor and do all thy work; but the seventh day is the Sabbath in honor of the Lord thy God; on it thou shalt not do any work, neither thou, nor thy son, nor thy daughter, thy man-servant, nor thy maid-servant, nor thy cattle, nor the stranger that is within thy gates. For in six days the Lord made the heavens and the earth, the sea, and all that is in them, and rested on the seventh day; therefore the Lord blessed the Sabbath Day, and hallowed it."— *Fourth Commandment.*

Jehovah entrusted to Moses the two tables of stone on which were graven the Ten Commandments. These edicts were the basic law of the ancient Jews. And so faithfully have they been observed throughout the passing centuries that on Saturday in a strictly orthodox Hebrew family none of its members will so much as build a fire on the coldest winter day. We can understand why it is that the Jewish Sabbath still remains— Saturday, the seventh day.

But the Christians received their fundamental religious laws from Christ, himself a Jew. How comes it

31

then that these sects have set apart as their day of
rest not the seventh but the first day of the week—
Sunday?

That sprang from another old custom of the
Hebrews. The Sabbath was the Lord's day; it was
not to be defiled. And in their view a corpse represented defilement. Burials never take place from a
Jewish synagogue; the dead are not permitted to
enter the house of the Lord. Nor will a devout Jew
in any way minister to a corpse on Saturday. According to the Hebrew method of reckoning time, Saturday begins with sundown on Friday and lasts until
the following sunset.

The Crucifixion, you remember, took place on Friday, and it was towards the close of the day when the
Nazarene's body was taken down from the Cross. St.
Mark tells us, "And now when the even was come,
because it was the preparation, that is, the day before
the Sabbath, Joseph of Arimathea, an honorable coun-
cillor, which also waited for the kingdom of God, came,
and went in boldly unto Pilate, and craved the body of
Jesus." Joseph, himself a pious Jew, wished to have
the Savior's body taken care of before the arrival of
the Sabbath—before sundown—to avoid breaking the
Mosaic law.

On Saturday there was no attempt on the part of
Christ's Jewish followers to disturb the body. These
people had been reared to attend no corpse on the

32

Sabbath, and lifelong habit is not easily violated; besides, in time of sudden catastrophe the mind is paralyzed and follows its customary procedure without conscious thought. In all likelihood the idea never occurred to even one of Christ's adherents to violate the ritualistic respect for the Sabbath Day by going in to the Presence that lay in Joseph's own new tomb, which he had hewn out in the rock. In fact, the tomb had been hastily closed, you recall.

So Christ was buried on Friday. And He rose on Sunday.

Thereupon Sunday, the first day of the week, became of vast import to the disciples of Jesus. It was not long before they began to gather on that day in commemoration of the Ascension. As the actual moment receded farther and farther in time its observance took on more and more of the sacred character of the Man Who had made it hallowed. Religious services began to be held by the Christians on the day of the week when the Ascension took place. These grew in length and in magnitude. Soon a great part of the entire day was devoted to church exercises, and secular matters were given scant or no attention. In time Saturday lost its original significance to the Christians, while Sunday became the day of rest and of religious meditation.

This change received authority from the acts and statements of Jesus. We recall that "Man was not made for the Sabbath, but the Sabbath was made for

33

man." Again, "The Son of Man is Lord even of the Sabbath Day." And when the afflicted crept to Christ begging to be helped He healed them though it was on the Sabbath, thereby incurring the ill-will of many who did not appreciate His viewpoint. So the disciples and those with them enjoyed ample precedent of the kind that would be most convincing to them that the old-time Sabbath might be disregarded in a proper manner.

That is why the Christian churches will be filled with worshipers on the first day of next week instead of the seventh.

WHY LADIES USE ROUGE

BEFORE me lies the report of a group of wise and serious archæologists. These men have been spending several years and thousands of dollars to dig into the earth-mounds that remain to mark the site of ancient Carthage. And from the whole sixty-four pages the one fact which stands out most humanly piteous to my mind is the discovery of a young girl's skeleton, buried in that far-off day, with her rouge pot beside her.

Another reverend galaxy of scientists has been unearthing the home-city of Abraham, Ur of the Chaldees. Gravely their records, reported by our daily journals, tell of finding this entrancing object and that, indicative of the life-customs of those long-vanished men and women. Again is mentioned the recovery of a little alabaster jar—and in its bottom, dried and darkened with age, still clings a pat of rouge.

Most of us read accounts of the sorting out of some of the curious and gorgeous relics drawn from the tomb of King Tut. He must have been a sweet-scented specimen of masculinity—if one may judge from the fact that apparently only his most cherished possessions were sealed up with his mummy and among them is a toilet jar of rouge! Can't you just see that young boy-king, still in his teens, draped in fine linen and purple, glittering with golden ornaments, strutting with his own importance, tawny of skin—and his cheeks flaming red? Whatever the king does always becomes the style, and it must have been a monstrously profitable business to be a rouge-merchant along the banks of the Nile in those days, five thousand three hundred years ago.

Rouge, rouge, rouge—red, red, red! For, indeed, the word rouge is but the French way of saying red. Why this universal passion for reddening the cheeks? We find traces of the custom as far back into antiquity as our knowledge will carry us and it exists quite as strongly today among many races. I have myself seen an Indian offer two arrows for either blue or yellow paint; but bow, quiver and nine arrows for a smaller quantity of red. Our own ladies would laugh heartily at the absurdity of painting their faces green or purple or brown, yet collectively they pay out a million dollars a day for beauty services and cosmetics—and standing high in the list is rouge.

Why red? Why everywhere the same color, applied in the same place?

We find the answer, I believe, in the "Personal Narrative" of the great traveler, Humboldt. He cites a great many examples to prove his conviction that man

36

admires and often tries to exaggerate whatever characters Nature may have given him.

Thus beardless nations, like the old Aztecs, took great pains to remove every trace of hair from the face and sometimes from the body as well. During the age of Attila, the Huns, who had flat broad noses like the Chinese, used to flatten the noses of their babies with bandages in order to increase this natural tendency. It is said that this holds true of the Malays of Sumatra, the Hottentots, certain Negro tribes of Africa and the natives of Brazil. Again, the Chinese have by nature exceptionally small feet; and it is widely known that the women of the upper classes compress their feet with bandages from infancy to comply with this character, often with such success that walking becomes almost impossible.

Many more instances might be cited, but these few will indicate the world-wide prevalence among us to value and to increase any racial peculiarity which may be apparent in the bodily structure. Returning now to our rouge, do we not find the basic cause for its use becoming obvious? Are not the cheeks of our women naturally red? Do we not admire red cheeks? Then if red cheeks attract the men, why not make them a teeny weeny bit redder?

A curious confirmation of this view is found in the fact that only those nations whose skin is light enough to permit the cheek color to be visible have used rouge.

Among the dark Negro races of Africa, for example, it would be difficult to find even one which has used red paint in the sense that we are now discussing. The reason, of course, is that the skin is so dark that no ruby tint could possibly show through from underneath; these savages have no idea that in lighter-skinned races the cheeks are pink. So the idea of increasing by artificial means a tint that they didn't know existed has never entered their heads.

Further support is lent to this view by the fact that our ladies use lipstick—another device to heighten the natural color of a visible part. But red is not the only color employed. We Caucasians admire white-skinned women, so our sisters and wives and sweethearts use powder to enhance their natural whiteness.

I cannot close this chapter without adding a few more examples of the esteem in which races hold their natural peculiarities of appearance. Thus when Park visited certain Negro tribes who had never seen a white man they were highly amused at his white skin and the prominence of his nose, both of which they considered decidedly unsightly disfigurements. Another white man, the first to be seen by some Negro boys, was derisively likened to a "white ape." Yet these same Africans considered their own quite black color most attractive; and one of the titles of the Zulu king, according to Mungo Park, is "You who are black."

Among the American Indians the hair ordinarily

38

grew to a great length, and among many tribes it was the custom to plait other substances in it to make it appear even longer; and so, too, the women of some African tribes make their woolly mops appear still more bushy by artificial means.

Recently an American scientist brought to this country from Central America three albino Indians, and I have read that these were willing to leave their native land because their copper-colored neighbors held them in contempt for being white. When I related this to an American woman she confessed that she always has to shudder in the presence of an albino. Yet an albino is merely one who has no color in hair, skin or eyes.

According to Madame Pfeiffer, in Java a girl is considered a beauty if she is yellow, and not white. Chinese have more than once been quoted as finding the white skin of our women too pale for their liking.

We may agree, then, that there is much truth in the saying that beauty is only skin deep; in fact, this statement is a bit too generous, for of the skin's four layers it is only the outer one which is seen. Truly this is a most delicate surface on which to base a judgment—but quite sufficient, as I am sure all my lady friends will admit. And, since they are such effective experts in the use of the skin and what to put on it, thus attracting skeptical men in shoals, I am quite content to be on their side and let the rest of the world think what it pleases.

WHY WE TIP THE HAT

I N the Martian *Daily News*, published on our neighboring planet under date of today, we might find perhaps a paragraph something like this:

"Our reporter, now visiting the Earth, sends us his curious story by wireless. We refrain from printing it without further verification, as his statements are so self-contradictory that we are confident static has garbled the message. For example, he says in part, 'I was walking down the street with one of the male inhabitants of Earth and as we passed a female whom he knew he removed his hat momentarily. Upon being asked why he performed this strange rite he explained that he did it as a token of respect. An hour later, having transported myself by radio to another part of this globe, called the Orient, I noted groups of males entering a building in which they worship, and each removed his shoes but kept on his hat. Upon inquiry I was assured that they do this as a token of respect.' Obviously, we submit, these diametrically opposite observances are impossible of belief."

Yet the reporter from Mars would be quite correct. Mankind does just those things, and precisely for the reason quoted. Maybe if we enlighten our foreign visitor on the origin of those customs he can set at rest the doubts of his managing editor.

Among the brutes as well as with mankind cowering or crouching appears to be an instinctive gesture of fear or inability to resist. All of us remember seeing strange dogs meet. The smaller and more timid, with lowered head and tail tucked quiveringly between the legs, awaits in evident dread the approach of his stiff-legged and determined antagonist. As the latter draws near, the submissive dog droops lower and lower, finally rolling over on his back, with legs helplessly folded. Always the conqueror understands this action. With a contemptuous sniff or two he walks away. Never does he attack. He knows there is no need.

This forcible illustration is offered for those who have not witnessed one man abasing himself before another. To an American, accustomed to self-respect, there is something sickening in the sight of a fellow-man casting himself prostrate into mud and filth and kissing the very dust that animals have trampled, in an abandonment of terror and humiliation. Yet during the Czarist days the peasants of Siberia so degraded themselves before a noble.

Trustworthy accounts of the days in our own South before the Civil War picture only too vividly how the whip-fearing colored slaves under a cruel master cringed and slunk. Always has this been true where slavery existed. And most of the conquering nations of the world, having discovered a source of cheap labor in prisoners of war, have been slave-owners during one part of their history. We can understand, then, how the crouching of the body universally betokened in the slave an acknowledgment of the presence of his master. This posture, adopted first instinctively, soon became demanded; the slave who dared to stand upright before his superior was given a prompt and unforgettable lesson. We can almost hear the brutal overseer threaten, as he grabs up a club, "I'll teach you to show *me* the proper respect, blast you."

So the cringing body would naturally become an accepted mark of respect. Pretty soon the common run of slaves would be bowing deeply before the old head-slaves. The slave-drivers would be making obeisance before their lords. Commoners would so greet chiefs. It was only a slight step from that to the familiar sign of submission being exchanged between equals, as when we step back politely at an elevator door and suggest to another, "After you, sir." Thus in the Bible we read of Jacob that when he saw his brother Esau coming, "he bowed himself to the ground seven times."

So an instinct became a custom.

In time, of course, this ceremonial would tend to grow less elaborate, and today a mere nod among acquaintances is all that is left of it in civilized countries. But it was always the head, you will notice, that

42

was inclined, either with the rest of the body or by itself.

Then men discovered armor. In the presence of his superior officer the ordinary soldier would indicate his inferiority by removing his protecting helmet. Until the day that armor was laid aside forever no man dared appear helmeted before his king. Again habit became custom, and when equals met each knight removed his metal casque out of respect to the other.

When gunpowder rendered armor useless the iron nutshell helmet became extinct, but the customary observances remained. Men now removed their hats before an equal or a superior, of either sex. Among certain nationalities, notably those of Latin ancestry, it is still considered polite for men to tip their hats to each other when meeting or parting.

But among the Semitic nations and their neighbors religious forms had crystallized long before the use of metal armor became common. In ancient Judea men might appear in negligée only before their intimates; honored guests found their host fully clad in ceremonial raiment, just as we today attire ourselves formally for the reception of respected visitors. Those men would no more have thought of presenting themselves in the synagogue or the mosque without a hat than we would consider going to church in our shirt-sleeves. What constituted a mark of respect to highly esteemed men served as a mark of respect to God. Yes, they did

43

Why We Do It

remove their shoes—but that was to avoid bringing the dust of unholy ground into the sanctuary.

The visitor from Mars, I fear, is not a very close observer. Our salute to a lady does not consist of merely raising the hat. There are two distinct actions. We first bare the head—because our ancestors were armored knights. And then we bow—because our still remoter ancestors kept slaves.

WHY WE HAVE HAT BANDS

YOU have a radio, of course. You turn the little knob ever so slightly and presto! you let me listen to Pittsburgh or Atlanta. Another turn of a degree or two and you transport me to St. Louis—Kansas City—Chicago—Cincinnati—seemingly to whatever city you prefer. Wonderful? Yes, indeed. I agree. But now see the little instrument that I have.

Your radio, remarkable as it is in reaching out into space, has yet the limitation of time. It can bring to my ears only what is going on right now, at this moment. But my hypothetical instrument will do more than that. It will carry you and me about—and not alone in space but in time also. It will take us anywhere and turn back the pages of time one year, two years, thr—here, try it yourself. Turn this red dial to point 62 and——

Hush! His Honor will have you ejected. What? Why, we are now in Dayton, Tenn., attending the famous evolution trial which happened several years ago. Yes, that is the judge up there on the high bench. Those men sitting within the enclosure in their shirt-sleeves fanning themselves are the lawyers. That one there—

45

no, don't point—that one is Clarence Darrow. And across from him, wiping the perspiration from his face and brow, is William Jennings Bryan. Take off your coat, if you like. It's hot enough to roast Beelzebub himself, isn't it? And how the droning big blue flies buzz and float across the court-room, glad to be indoors protected from the flickering heat-shimmer outside! Those overalled unshaven hill-billies in blue shirts crowded together as spectators don't seem to mind it, though. Wonder who they are.

What! Anti-evolutionists? Why, they all have a hat, don't they? I didn't hear you. What has a hat to do with evolution? My boy, my boy! Lend me your pencil. I'll sketch the first hat that was ever manufactured for mankind. Here it is.

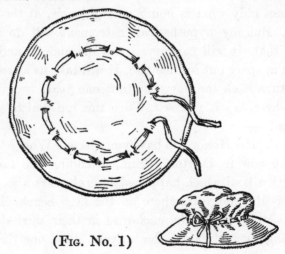

(FIG. No. 1)

Why We Have Hat Bands

Just a circular piece of leather, you see, with a circle of slits cut within it. A flat thong of leather was passed through the slits, pulled down to fit the wearer's head-size, and tied in a bow. And there was your hat.

(Fig. No. 2)

Rather a makeshift, I agree, but for all that you will note in its shape a certain resemblance to the plumed and velvet headgear of Queen Elizabeth's time. Yes, this first crude hat had a number of drawbacks, which have been gradually eliminated during the centuries.

First of all, this leather hat would naturally be quite limp. The brim would flap down over the eyes in most annoying fashion, unless we should find some way to brace it up. In pictures of old-timers of the pre-Renaissance period you've seen one such method of bracing—a ribbon starting over each ear, carried out to

47

the edge of the brim and then brought up outside and tied in a bow over the crown of the hat. That worked very well. Every once in a while such a ribbon or thong would pull loose from its moorings; and then it was discovered that a brim which had been kept curled up at its edge for a long time would retain that shape; it would stay curled, like the brim of a cowboy's hat where he holds it to keep it from blowing off in a high wind. From that it was only a step to omit the bracing thong entirely, curling the edge of the brim by hand. Borrow that old Fedora from the sun-tanned mountaineer next to you. Thanks. This will do excellently. It has the brim curled up all around, you notice. It was made so at the factory. Of course, by our modern methods of hat manufacture this curl is hardly necessary any more, for we now have means of stiffening the brim if we care to use them. But the first hats had their brims curled; and even though a curled brim is a rain-catcher, you and I must go on wearing them just because several centuries ago hat-makers were unable to stiffen a leather disc.

Cut leather has a raw edge. So after a time these leather hats began to fray and grow ragged where the knife had passed through. That was easy enough for an ingenious man to hide, of course, so the hatters of those days cut a strip of thin leather or cloth and bound it around the raw edge. There's a band of ribbon sewed around the edge of this gentleman's brim, isn't there?

48

Why We Have Hat Bands

Another hang-over from the old times. A few of our modern felt hats are made without this edge-binding, proving that we can do without it. But, no—hats have always had binding, so ours must be bound, too!

Let us go back to the picture of the leather hat. Where the thong fitted around the head it wove in and out of the slits; it showed on the outside in little strips, giving the effect of a band. Has this hat which we borrowed from the gentleman a band? It certainly has. Not only that, but notwithstanding that this modern hat will fit only one size of head it still has the old leather thong's bow—as if tightening or loosening this band could make the hat fit better! Nowadays the bow is often made elaborate and turned into an ornament, but we see where it had its utilitarian origin.

This bow, please mark, is on the left hand side. That is where you always see the hat-bow. Oh, yes, once in a while you'll find a hat-maker in the search for novelty swinging the bow around to the back, but seldom indeed do you notice many such hats worn. That style never seems to take. Irresistibly the bow seems to creep right back to the left side. Never to the right; never to the front. Always to the left. But why? There must be a reason for that.

There is. A short while ago we mentioned the velvet plumed hats of the dandies in the ancient courts of England and France. Their plumes often swept majestically down over the edge of the brim. But those bedizened young gallants wore other things besides a plume—for example, a sword. Nor was that rapier just for show; they used its razor-sharp blade; that was part of their daily business, almost. And when a man is fighting for his life he doesn't want a foot or so of ostrich feather dangling before his eyes.

Being right-handed, most of them, those perfumed duelists advanced the right side of the body in fencing. If the plume were on the left it would thus be thrown back out of the way, where it would not interfere with sight. Naturally, then, those valorous gentlemen had their plumes attached on the left side, with a silken bow or buckle. Wherefore this Tennesseean's bow, you observe, is also on the left, though he doesn't know the reason for it.

Once the thong had suggested a band it did not take the vain courtiers of those days long to improve on the idea. They flaunted bands of crushed velvet, or rare Turkey damask, or even jeweled cloth of gold. That hid the thong, which had now become a cord or tie-string, except when the hat was looked at from the inside. The fancy outer band still had its bow or buckle at the left and it would hardly do to pile one bow over the other. So the knot of the tie-string was cut down to the smallest possible size and worked around to the back where it would cause the least discomfort. It would be hidden under the band, remember. Let us examine the inside of the gentleman's hat. Yes, here it is. See

50

the little white silk bow back here where the edges of the sweat-band meet? And notice, please, how the two ribbons which form the bow are laced in and out through slits cut into the leather. Solomon was right—there's nothing new under the sun!

That's about all there is to the hat, except the lining. When velvet hats took the place of those made of leather some protection was required to keep the soft-falling velvet from contact with the oil and perspiration of the scalp, so cloth linings were used. This felt hat has enough body to stand up; it will never crumple down onto the gentleman's pate, but the lining is there just the same, evolved from a past necessity which has all but passed out of memory. I shall return the gentleman his property.

Sir, let us thank you for lending us your hat. I have just been explaining to my friend here why the brim is curled, why the edge is bound with ribbon, why the hat includes a band, why the bow shows on the left, why the interior bears a lining and why the sweat-band is finished with a little bow in the back. Sir? How did we enjoy the trial? The trial? Which tri—oh, good land, we have been so absorbed in tracing the evolution of the hat that we actually forgot we were in Dayton! Silly of us, wasn't it?

WHY WE SEND FLOWERS
TO FUNERALS

THE fight was over. Old One-Eye, the Stone Age bully, had picked a quarrel once too often. This time a stalwart stripling had banged him effectually over the head with a club and One-Eye had gone down, never to rise again.

The women of his household began the usual ritualistic wailing. Intermingled with the custom-born cries of ostensible grief from some of them lay a very real worry. What was to become of them now? And who would provide for the children? Old One-Eye might have been hot of temper and heavy of hand but he at least brought home meat to eat, and hides to wear and lie upon.

And what to do with One-Eye's possessions, which had always been taboo, not to be touched by any except the owner? Was somebody else to take them now? What retribution would One-Eye's ghost wreak if that were permitted?

The problems were solved in simple fashion by the victor. He gathered into his own family young mothers from One-Eye's family; these brought along their chil-

dren, of course. The old women offered no attractions
to the conqueror; they could be left to starve, for all
of him. Naturally they had different notions about
that; so they buried what was left of One-Eye, ap-
peasing him by placing in the grave his spear, his bow
and arrows, his hide-blanket and all the things that
had been his. That would at least give his ghost implements for use in the "other" world, and keep it from
being vengeful; for as he had been powerful over his
people in life he might also have some power over them
now that he was dead. Anyway, they were taking no
chances.

The winner of the fatal battle offered no objection
to the burial of One-Eye's property; he feared to
appropriate it—he wanted no trouble with the dead
man's ghost.

In such manner, far back in the history of the race,
we are told, there arose the practice of burying with
the dead the articles that they had cared for in life.
The procedure has originated independently in many
widely separated parts of the world. Sometimes it has
been carried to barbarous extremes.

Thus in India, for example, a *sati* was a "good
woman." The wife who was so infatuated with her
husband, so faithful to him that she preferred to die
with him rather than to survive, was truly a *sati*. So—
the usual mode of disposal of the dead being by burning—when a wife threw herself upon her husband's

funeral pyre to be consumed with him she proved herself a *sati* beyond question. From a mispronunciation of this word the English have adopted the term *suttee* to describe the widow's self-sacrifice by fire.

A similar procedure took place in the Fiji Islands, separated from India by such vast expanses of ocean that the inhabitants of the two places had probably never heard of each other until the coming of the white men. So strong was the Fijian public opinion on this point that the widow who refused to be burned with her dead spouse was an abhorred outcast for the remainder of her life; and the first Christian missionaries were dumbfounded when they discovered that their efforts to rescue the widow met with invariable resistance on her part; she found it easier to die than to live under the stigma of a violated ritual.

Not so long ago the burial ship of a Viking was uncovered, and in it were found the skeletons of men and women, as well as animals, all sacrifices at the funeral of their lord. King Tut-Ankh-Amen's tomb was crammed full of the most gorgeous relics, all one-time possessions of the deceased monarch. The American Indians, the Tatars and other tribes used to slay and bury with dead men the horses and dogs that the deceased had owned in this life.

The reason behind all these varied rites was the same—the belief that things as well as living beings had ghosts; and that the spirits of persons, animals

54

and objects sacrificed at the grave of the dead accompanied him to the other life, there to perform for him the same functions as here. The list could be extended to great length, and is decidedly interesting; but we have need to take up our immediate subject.

As races became more civilized their views underwent changes, of course; that itself is partly the reason for civilization, partly its effect. By slow stages the sacrifices grew fewer; the more valuable—such as human and animal lives—being the first to be preserved. Even today, though, some European peasants put a coin on the eyes or between the lips of the corpse, that he may be able to pay the ferry-man to take him across the River of Death, beyond which lies the Happy Land. The Chinese scatter along the route of the funeral procession bits of gilt and silver paper that the demons may be so busily engaged in gathering this "money" that they will be kept eagerly occupied until the interment—after which the dead man's ghost will be safe from fiendish attack. These gilt and silver paper discs are doubtless now symbolic relics of actual money formerly used for this purpose; just as the beds, and chairs, and ducks, and horses and other articles belonging to the dead man, now buried with their owner in the form of small paper cut-outs for the sake of economy, are a reminder of the days when the objects themselves went into the grave.

So we have three well-marked stages of offerings to

the dead; the actual object, its substitute in various forms, and—finally—mere tributes of respect.

Now, among many distinct races flowers have been used to symbolize purity; and it is no cause for wonder that so far back as 1636 William Sampson could write,

> "Those smelling sweetes with which our sense
> was fed
> Were for the burial of a maiden, dead."

Long before this, however, flowers were employed as funeral offerings, but only in the case of virgins. Gradually the custom expanded; until today, still feeling the urge to offer something to our departed friends, we send flowers, without regard to sex or marital condition.

Dirges at funerals descend to us from a custom of the ancient Irish, who employed noises as the Chinese of the present day utilize cymbals and tom-toms—to frighten away hungry and attendant demons. In time the barbarous drumming and clashing of metal gave way to softer and less offensive sounds—music.

From our good friends the Irish we received also the term "wake," used to describe the present-day shrunken form of the ancient funeral feast—another custom which is practically world-wide in its extent, and which was known to the Egyptians, the Romans, and other nations of antiquity to whom we are indebted for the current aspects of many of our rites.

Why We Send Flowers to Funerals

So old One-Eye's soul turned into a bad and harmful and fearsome spirit; the soul of the Chinese is good, though it is threatened by evil shades which yet can be tempted away before they do mischief; that of our own dead rests peacefully and untroubled with God. By such stumbling steps as these has mankind at last arrived at a confident faith in its Creator.

WHY WE LIKE PUZZLES

MRS. ARCHIMEDES, wife of the great Greek mathematician, was attending a meeting of the Tuesday Musical Club in Syracuse, Sicily, in the year 250 B. C. Among the guests was Mrs. Psammetichus, an Egyptian lady from Alexandria, who had known Archimedes in his youth, and was consequently the object of the jealous suspicion of Mrs. Archimedes. The latter, however, having captured the prize, felt inclined to chasten her rival; so she began, "Have you read my husband's latest book, 'The Quadrature of the Parabola'? He likes it ever so much better than even his 'Conoids and Spheroids,' or his 'Measurements of the Circle,' or his 'Equilibrium of Planes,' or any of his other works. And King Hiero thinks the world and all of him. He's the cleverest man!"

And Mrs. Psammetichus, being likewise a cat, rejoined, "But he's so queer. I just saw him running down the street without any clothes on." Whereupon Mrs. Archimedes set off for home.

On her arrival she saw the philosopher in the kitchen, stark nude, fiddling with two of her best baking pans; water was slopped all over the floor. She said, "Well!"

Why We Like Puzzles

Archimedes looked up with a happy grin. "Eureka!" he remarked. "I've got it!"

"No," returned Mrs. Archimedes. "Not yet, you haven't; but you're going to get it. What's the idea of this display? Of all the—— What'll the neighbors think?"

"The neighbors?" murmured her husband, busily immersed in his problem again. "What neighbors? Oh, the neighbors be—be blowed! There isn't one of 'em could do it."

"Not one of them could do it!" gasped his spouse. "Which of 'em would want to do it, will you tell me? Where are your clothes?"

"I left them at the bath-house."

"At the bath-house? Land sakes! What for?"

"I was in a hurry."

"In a hur—— I'll say you were. You go right into your room and put on some clothes. Then you come back here. I want to talk to you."

What had excited the mathematical genius was this: King Hiero had ordered a golden crown. When it came he conceived an idea that maybe he'd been gold-bricked. So he said to Archimedes, "Here, Arch, help me out. I want to know whether there is some silver mixed into the metal of this crown. It's beautiful, I admit—the prettiest thing I ever saw. If it's pure gold I wouldn't have it harmed for anything. So don't go to digging out little pieces of it to assay. What I want you to do

59

is to discover whether there is any silver in it without removing even a trace of the metal."

And Archimedes replied, "What the—oh, all right. Lemme think it over for a few days." It was while he was wrestling with this assignment that he went to the public baths. In stepping into his tub, which had been filled to the brim, he noticed that a quantity of water overflowed. Instantly the thought came to him, "If to a vessel full of water I add pure gold exactly equal to the crown in weight and measure the overflow; and if I fill the vessel again and immerse the crown and measure that overflow, then if there's any difference between the two overflows there's been some funny work done on that crown. Eureka!" And he ran off home to test it out, leaving his clothes behind in the excitement.

That, at least, is the story told to us by his contemporaries. But maybe it is all a press-agent stunt to account for the fact that Archimedes jumped out of the tub and refused to bathe at all. This seems especially plausible when we consider that there is no record of Archimedes' having been in a bath before or since that memorable occasion. Whether a man who would run through the streets clad only in his enthusiasm is the type that would practice regular ablutions is a matter for the reader to decide.

But the story does illustrate vividly one very human trait—the love of puzzles. There appears to be a streak of perversity in all of us which responds to the implied

60

challenge, "You can't do it," with the defiance, "Bet you I can." Almost nobody is immune. The only person I ever met who disregarded a puzzle was a staid, conservative Wall Street banker in whose office I was waiting one day to lunch with him. While he was signing some checks I pulled out a little contrivance of two twisted wires and tried to undo them. He kept his attention on the checks. And I was surprised. Yet after we had eaten and the cigars were lit he remarked, "Maybe I could get 'em apart. Lemme see it."

Everybody has racked his brains over cross-word puzzles. And for what? When one was finished the only reward was having done it. Who hasn't spent hours with a little circular glass-topped device attempting to get the mouse into the trap? Or fitting blocks of wood into all sorts of combinations trying to move the big square from corner A down to corner B without lifting a piece? Or finding the two cats hidden in the leaves of the tree? Or drawing three straight lines to pen fourteen bees so that only two will be in any one enclosure? Or finding what is wrong with this picture?

Two of the schoolboys next door brought in a problem to me one night to be solved. It was a tough one, they admitted. I had already started this chapter; so, like Archimedes, I had a thought. "Boys," I suggested, "before we start on that example, let's solve this puzzle in the World's 'Red Magic.' Here it is: 'Two ferryboats start from opposite sides of the river at the same

61

instant and meet 720 yards from the nearest shore.
They remain in their respective slips ten minutes, and
on the return trip meet 400 yards from the other shore.
How wide is the river?' "

In a few minutes one of them cried, "I have it!" Not
being a Greek mathematician he didn't cry, "Eureka!"
and he kept his shirt on. But he had found the answer.
So I pointed out that this was essentially the same
problem as the teacher had set; in a trice both boys
had solved the given problem. There we have it—as a
school example its solution involved brain-taxing to
complete a duty and that is always work; but as a
puzzle the brain-taxing was incidental to proving that
"I can do it," and that was fun.

We Americans are not the only folks who enjoy puzzles or riddles—for a riddle, of course, is just a verbal
puzzle. Among primitive peoples the riddle is imme-
morially old, and is used by them not only to sharpen
their own wits but to exercise the brains of their little
ones as well. A few samples may prove interesting.

"Guess ye some men who are many and form a row,"
propounds the Zulu; "they dance the wedding dance,
adorned in white hip-dresses." To which the answer
with its attendant comments is, "The teeth; we call
them men who form a row, for the teeth stand like men
who are made ready for a wedding-dance, that they may
dance well. When we say, they are 'adorned with white
hip-dresses,' we put that in that people may not at

once think of teeth but be drawn away from them by thinking, 'It is men who put on white hip-dresses,' and continually have their thoughts fixed on men."

Among the Basutos riddles are a recognized part of education and are set like exercises to a whole company of puzzled children. *Q.* "Do you know what throws itself from the mountain-top without being broken?" *A.* "A waterfall." *Q.* "There is a thing that travels fast without legs or wings, and no cliff, nor river, nor wall can stop it." *A.* "The voice." This one, I fancy, should prove easy even for children: *Q.* "Name the ten trees with ten flat stones on top of them." *A.* "The fingers." And this one gives us a quick glimpse into a novel Basuto custom: *Q.* "Who is the little immovable dumb boy who is dressed up warm in the day and left naked at night?" *A.* "The bed-clothes' peg."

From Samoa: *Q.* "A white-headed man stands above the fence, and reaches to the heavens." *A.* "The smoke of the oven." From old Mexico: "What is it we get into by three parts and out of by one?" "A shirt." Another from the same source reminds us of our own nursery rhyme: "What goes through a valley and drags its entrails after it?" The answer is the same as to, "Old Mother Twitchett she had but one eye, And a long tail which she let fly; And every time she went over a gap, She left a bit of her tail in a trap." Though how anybody could fairly expect a child to guess, "A needle," as the answer to either is beyond me.

63

Why We Do It

Yet children delight in riddles. I know of my own experience that an ailing child can be comforted and amused for an hour or more with them. When we find a custom of such distinct nature scattered all over the world and in high favor among our own youngsters we may have good reason to suspect a profound natural instinct at the root. And this I believe is the case.

Man, with his weak and vulnerable body unfitted for defence and lacking natural weapons, like tusks or claws, was for generation after generation in prehistoric times exposed to constant dangers. He had but one possible superiority over the brute creation which surrounded him—his brain. He had to outwit his prey for he could not successfully pursue; he had to outwit his pursuers or be preyed on and prayed for. Hence every means of exercising and strengthening his mental powers was of excellent service to him. The riddle is a simple method of putting a keen edge on the mind, and its practical variations are endless. Savage man everywhere has hit upon this superb grindstone for sharpening his wit, and our children have inherited the joy of it. We, ourselves, heartily appreciate a new puzzle until its novelty wears off.

Proof? Well, previously I mentioned the puzzle of the two ferry-boats. It can be worked by simple arithmetic. The answer is this: the width of the river—but perhaps you'll prefer puzzling it out for yourself.

WHY WE HAVE COATS

IT was a cold, sleety mid-day back in the Stone Age. Overhead swung huge gray-bellied clouds, scudding before the wind, darkening the earth beneath them. The towering trees, already stripped of their summer foliage, bowed every now and then as a fiercer gust than usual whistled through their naked branches. With the wind-swirls came the rattling patter of scattering ice-beads. And beneath one of the larger trees old One-Eye, husband of Short-Hair, stood shivering.

Naked was One-Eye, except for his coarse flowing locks and his long beard. He stood first on one foot, then on the other, his shoulders hunched up about his neck to keep off the wind. In his hands he held his bow and three arrows. Under his left arm he hugged a flint knife. His little black eyes, gleaming specks below bushy brows, peered ravenously as he turned his head from side to side in search of prey. One-Eye was not only cold; he was hungry. The hunting had not been good for several days past. The last bone in his cave had been gnawed bare. One-Eye wanted meat.

What? Had he heard something just before that last swoop of wind had cut off the sound with its shrill zwee-ee? He listened again in the lull. Yes, there it was—a buzzing droning hum. Hastily he glanced around him. Nothing moved. Yet the sound continued. One-Eye's gooseflesh began to prickle. Danger! He huddled. Then came the hum again. One-Eye straightened and laughed. Wild bees in the tree-trunk behind him, swarming for the coming winter. He longed for some of the honey that he knew was there. But he feared the hot sharp stings of the bees. He remembered . . . once before . . . the autumn when Four-Fingers and he had hunted together last. . . . Ooh, how bees could sting!

Hark! A twig crackled. One-Eye crouched to earth. What was it? Where was it? The beady black eyes flickered everywhere at once. Was—could it be—the—yes! Behind that bush. Something big and brown. He smelled it now—the musty heavy smell that one sometimes encountered in empty caves. Ha! One-Eye was in luck. The smell of the honey had drawn the thing hither.

Slowly, oh, ever so slowly, he fitted one of the arrows that he was holding in his left hand to the string of the bow in his right. Clamping that arrow with his fingers he laid the other two softly on the ground, so deliberately that he seemed not to move. Then, slowly, slowly, the left hand crept up. It grasped the arching bow at the middle. Three fingers crept around the wooden curve, the index finger pointing out straight

66

ahead as a sight, the thumb shoved over underneath the arrow to serve it as a rest.

One-Eye was hardly breathing now. His little black eyes were burning. Except for his tight-closed lips, twitching in excitement, he seemed not to move. Yet up, up, up the left hand crept—and back, back, back inched the right. The bow was bending now. Softly, gently One-Eye increased the tension, the right hand creeping ever farther and farther back. He could see the sparkle of two eyes as the beast behind the bush gazed and gazed at him. Swoo-oo-oosh! Another spray of sleet brushed around One-Eye, shielding him momentarily from the thing behind the bush; and in that precious instant his two hands spread far apart. His back-muscles became hard with the taut pull of the straining bow. Patter, patter, patter! The ice-beads scattered and fell. Came a lull and—zoom! One-Eye released the arrow, grabbing his two remaining shafts and scrambling to his feet in case he had to fly. But, no; again he was in luck. The thing gave a deep, surprised, drawn-out grunt, thrashed about heavily among the crisp dead leaves and lay still. One-Eye's hands, he found, were almost numb from cold. And hungry! He licked his lips. But this might be a trap.

Warily he skirted around in a great circle, keeping trees between himself and the bush behind which lay the thing. Always he held his look fixed on the brown mass, his leg-muscles tightened for flight. Then, as he

Why We Do It

pushed his head out from the shelter of a great tree-trunk, he saw it lying clear. A bear! Resting flat on its side it was, his arrow spitted clean through the bulky body.

Caution gripped One-Eye. He had seen dead things rise and rip men open before this. He fixed another arrow, stretched his bow and tiptoed ahead, ready to shoot if necessary. But the bear was dead, really dead. One-Eye pushed it with his foot. Yes, it was dead. "Yee-ee-ee-eehooooooooooo!" Old One-Eye's yell of triumph echoed through the forest.

Greedily he felt his prize, the bow and arrows cast aside. From his armpit where he had carried it all this time he seized his flint-chipped knife. The bear was too heavy to carry home whole. So One-Eye lifted one fore paw, slit the stomach-hide from neck to tail and for the next hour he hacked and cut, removing the skin. Time and again he stopped to munch a mouthful of meat. At length he carved off and carried away a great hind-quarter. And because the sleet was falling faster now he threw the shaggy hide over his head and shoulders.

Twice during the following day he came, carving off and carrying away meat that the jackals had not devoured. Always he wore the skin over his shoulders to keep away the biting wind. Here was a good idea, wearing that hide! Between gorges he scraped and scraped at the inside of the skin, removing the stiffened membrane. It became somewhat pliable.

Why We Have Coats

But it kept slipping off. That was the trouble with it; One-Eye had to give over one hand to holding it in place on his shoulders. And where two hands are needed for bow and arrows there is no hand to hold a bearskin with. One-Eye hated to give it up. He squatted and spread the hide on the ground in front of him, admiring it. His eye lit on the hole near the middle where Short-Hair last night had let it fall into the fire in the cave and be burned. Well, she wouldn't do *that* any more. He could hear her sobbing fitfully yet, back in the cave a hundred feet away, recovering gradually from the whaling he had given her again this morning for it.

He held the skin up before him, peeping through the hole. This was fun. The closer he brought his head to the hole the wider became the vista before him. When he drew back the scene shrunk. He wondered how it would look if he stuck his head clear through. Trying it, he laughed. Then he tried it again, standing up. As he started to lift it off he heard a snap behind him. He jumped for his weapons, poised for flight or fight. But nothing happened. One-Eye, nervous, slunk away, the bearskin still hanging from his shoulders.

Back inside the cave Short-Hair was cuddled on the ground, her head hanging between her drawn-up knees. Still red were her eyes from weeping. As One-Eye barged in, his torso covered with bear hide, she edged fearsomely out of his way. But he wasn't angry at her any more. He beckoned her outside, and when she ventured timorously forth he stood up draped in the bearskin and laughed. She, sensing a truce, clapped her hands and laughed, too.

Then One-Eye danced in glee at his discovery. But he couldn't swing his arms. The heavy hide held them down. Grasping the flint knife from under his arm again he cut a slit in the skin from his left shoulder down to the hide's edge. Out through the slit came his left hand to cut another such slit below the right shoulder. Now his arms were free. And One-Eye had thought all this out himself. Truly he was a great man. He howled now as he danced—howled a pæan of self-praise.

It was on towards late spring before it occurred to One-Eye's neighbor, Long-Face, to don such a hide for himself. But when he did he added to it. One-Eye's hide left his arms free in front, but movement to the sides and rear were impeded by the weight of the pelt. Long-Face cut four slits in his deerskin covering—one in front of each arm, one in back. He could move his arms freely now.

But the drape over the shoulder flapped and caught in the underbrush. Long-Face's wife made him hold his arms out straight while she pinned the flapping ends together with thorns. Now her husband had sleeves. Only centuries later did the thought strike anyone to slit the hide open down the front and pin it together there, so as to make easy the donning and removal of it. Meanwhile Long-Face and One-Eye paraded in their sleeved skin-coats.

These were well enough as far as they went. But they left the legs exposed to thorns and cold. Another innovator, copying after One-Eye and Long-Face, not only wore a coat but wrapped another skin about his waist, covering his legs. This proved a vast betterment. And then some deep thinker, finding the hairy skirt too confining, slit it fore and aft between the legs, pinned the flapping edges together and lo—he had trousers.

Of course, as One-Eye and Long-Face made other killings and acquired new clean skins they gave their cast-off garments to their wives, generous souls that they were. After a time these women found that the trousers had disadvantages; for one thing they let the baby slip through when one held him on the lap. So the women wheedled uncut skins from their husbands, wore these tied about their waists and thus went back to skirts. Not all the women of the world disliked trousers. In Korea, for example, the women and the men both wore them, and do so until this day. But our own far-removed grandmothers preferred otherwise. When One-Eye saw this he called over to Long-Face in anguished amazement, "My gosh, the women are going to give up pants and wear skirts! Can you imagine that?"

In some such way as this did things come about in the Paleolithic Age. Old One-Eye sleeps in peace these many centuries with his forefathers. And we, arising in the morning from a soft warm bed, slip into our trousers of the latest cut, skim over the Women's Page in the daily paper, light upon an illustrated fashion item and exclaim to our wives, "My gosh! I see here that women are going to give up skirts and wear knickers—pants! Can you imagine that?"

From somewhere there comes a little snicker. It is the ghost of Short-Hair, tittering.

WHY WE EMPLOY DEAD PHRASES

EVERYONE recognizes that it is ill-bred to discuss our physical symptoms in company. But if it is good manners to ask, "How are you?" why isn't it good manners to answer with the truth? If it is polite for you to inquire, "How do you feel today?" it ought to be equally polite for me to reply, "I've got the tummy ache; and the temporary traumatic exostosis of the tibia concerning which I have been consulting Dr. Brown still manifests itself through a severe local vascular congestion. Uh-huh."

Can you imagine!

A friend is relating an incident which he considers interesting. He rattles on, "And I said . . . and she said . . . and I said . . . and she said . . ." Whereupon we courteously inquire, "Is that so?" To which, of course, the proper reaction would be, "Well, do you think I am fibbing?" Only, of course, nobody ever accepts the question as meaning what it really implies.

We invite Joe Smith and his wife up for dinner. The soup is cold, the chicken is tough, the dessert is loaded with whipped cream and Joe just detests rich food. After the meal we sit around for an hour trying to make conversation but nobody can think of any topic to arouse general interest; everyone is bored to distraction. To relieve the agony we suggest a game of bridge, which is poison to Joe, but he takes a hand because that is less intolerable than listening to a lot of aimless powwow, and during its course we relieve him of four dollars of his money. Gratefully he hears the clock strike eleven, and as he and his spouse part from us at the door they assure us blandly, "We've had a lovely time."

And we, wishing inwardly that we had been spared the misery of such a session, urge sweetly, "Do come again soon."

We know darn well that they did *not* have a good time. And, as for repeating the visit, as soon as Joe has slammed the door of his coupé he snarls at his wife, "Well, the next time you catch *me* coming to this——" and Mrs. Smith interrupts with, "Hush, Joe, they'll hear you," but she doesn't disagree.

In reading of the Tupis of Brazil we smile at their method of greeting a stranger. The visitor enters the hut and remains silent, waiting to be noticed. After a time the host decides to acknowledge his caller's presence and does so with the customary formula, "Art thou come?" We facetious Americans would be tempted to respond, "No; I'm on my way, though, and I'll be here in about an hour." The indigenous guest, however, is expecting just this greeting; when it comes he replies

with the habitual, "Yes, I am come." Doesn't that seem
queer to us?

Yet is it any sillier than what happens when I tele-
phone an Englishman's office? I tell his secretary my
name and I ask to speak to the employer. Then the man
I am waiting for picks up the receiver and inquires of
me, "Are you there?" Of course I'm there. How could
I have put through the call in the first place if I weren't
there? If I'm not there where does he think I am?

Let us not wax too sarcastic. How much more to the
point is our own custom of saying, "God be with you"
when we close the conversation? Oh, yes, we do say it;
only we have, after long usage, abbreviated its form
through various stages—God be with you, God b' wi'
ye, good-by. Time and again, day after day, we utter
that word, good-by, without even a passing thought
of the Deity. It is just as meaningless to us now as
"Have you come?" or "Are you there?" True, we
require some means of signifying that we have no
more to say, and we might fittingly indicate this with,
"I have finished." But no, the habit has been established and we keep it up as unthinkingly as the Tupis
and the English maintain their traditional forms.

Compare French *adieu* and Spanish *adios*.

The world hello, used in opening an American tele-
phone talk, is more defensible. In its original form it
was, "Hail to you," an obvious greeting. At that,
though, when we crisply snap, "Hello, Dick," it never

occurs to us that we are really voicing the sentiment, "Hail to you, Richard."

While we have been telephoning, a visitor has stepped into our office. We utter the usual formula, "Good morning." Why? Do we offer this as a comment on the weather, meaning, "This morning is a good one"? Indeed not; it is far from being a good morning, for the rain is beating down in torrents and threatens never to cease. Do we mean, "I hope you have a good morning"? Impossible, for it is already near mid-day and the morning is gone. Do we substitute, "Good day"? It is still raining pitchforks. Shall we ask, "How are you?" He might reply, "The temporary exostosis of the tibia———"

The fact is, of course, that we feel some sort of greeting necessary to indicate amiability. Certain phrases have become standardized, and we use those because everybody recognizes them for what they are. This would indeed be a rough and uncouth world if we eliminated the many forms which have come to be accepted as signifying respect and consideration for others.

These phrases and many others like them may have lost their original meaning but they still retain their original intent. Respect for ourselves demands that we display a similar respect for those with whom we mingle, for birds of a feather flock together and if our companions are unworthy of high regard we are no better. These marks of respect, extended to our close associates, soon broaden their range until we show a genteel courtesy in our treatment of all mankind. George Washington, when asked why he removed his hat to answer the salutation of a Negro, replied, "I cannot be outdone in politeness by a slave."

So as our civilization grows older we shall undoubtedly add more and more to the stock phrases employed in daily intercourse with our fellows. These phrases will lose their original sense, we may be sure, but each will nevertheless increase the outward show of human kindness which makes it possible for millions of people to live together happily. Every friendly trifle is another drop of lubricant on the wheels of the machinery of social progress.

WHY WE HAVE BARBER POLES

AT the close of "As You Like It" Rosalind de-
claims, "If it be true that good wine needs no
bush, 'tis true that a good play needs no epilogue."
In those times the epilogue was tag-ended onto every
play; it was a sort of "Thank you," to the audience,
a closing word of gratitude in behalf of actors and
author alike. Its purpose was much the same as that
of the signs we see occasionally, "If we please you tell
your friends; if not, tell us"; in other words, an advertisement. What connection did Shakespeare see between
the advertisement of a play and the "bush" of good
wine?

Haven't you noticed that many shoemakers' shops
display above the door a boot? Sometimes it is cut out
of sheet-metal, sometimes turned out of wood and
gilded. Often, too, we see the boot painted on the window. No matter what form it takes we always recognize
the sign as the mark of a shoemaker's business.

That sort of sign has one enormous advantage—
even the most ignorant can understand its message.
People who have never learned to read know that the
boot means, "Shoes repaired here." True, in almost

every case the man's name and the nature of his business are lettered in the show-window, too; so the picture would seem unnecessary. But we can be glad that the custom continues, for it brings into our own day a type of business sign which is nearly extinct, yet which was highly essential at one time, before reading was a common accomplishment.

You see, we are likely to forget that universal education is quite a new thing in this world. Here in America so many are able to read and write that one who finds these arts beyond his ability considers himself disgraced; his fellows look down on him. Yet in parts of Roumania you must count eight people before you find one who can read short easy words; in Russia six men scrawl a cross as their signature for every one who can painfully but proudly write even his name; among the Spaniards reading and writing are so rare that but one in five or six knows his letters. This, in a great measure, was true even in America until about fifty years ago. Only after the Civil War did schooling become really widespread among practically all the people of our land. And in a country where most of the people cannot read it is useless to print business signs.

So in past centuries the signs were pictures, just as those of the shoemakers are today. Sir John Falstaff took his ease at his inn known as the Boar's Head. The advertisement swinging in front of the hostelry did not read "B-O-A-R-S H-E-A-D." No; that wouldn't have done any good; nobody could have made out what it meant, except a few clerks and clerics. Instead, the wooden board displayed to the passer-by the painted head of a boar.

So, too, "The Three Georges" hung out the portraits of King George I and his two successors of the same name. "The Golden Slipper" had a sign that we can easily picture to ourselves. Sign-painters had but limited skill in those days and it would have been far beyond their art to paint a picture that would convey to the beholder such a firm name as B. Altman & Co., for instance, or Tiffany's. Therefore stores and taverns called themselves by paintable names, as "The Spinning Wheel," or "The Golden Ring," or "The Plume and Buckle," depending on whether they sold linen or jewelry or millinery.

Now, when an innkeeper received a shipment of new wine he announced the fact by nailing a leafy bough to his roof-tree, just as our carpenters used to do when the framework of a new house had been completed. In the case of the carpenters the bough meant that the owner was expected to furnish a keg of beer. That custom itself was descended from the practice of the innkeepers. In the olden days this leafy advertisement of newly-arrived tasty wine was called a "bush," because as often as not it was a real bush or spray of grape leaves instead of a tree-limb. We see now what Shakespeare meant when he said that "Good wine needs no bush." If the wine were good enough the customers would tell their friends; the bushy advertisement would be superfluous. In all likelihood the wine-drinkers, hearing of the news, would wear blisters on their feet getting to it in a hurry; and then they'd have to go to the barber to have their bruises given attention.

For even as far back as 454 A. D. Rome had barbers, and part of their duty was the extraction of teeth, the binding of wounds and other surgery. One of their chief activities in this line was "bleeding" patients, since until perhaps 150 years ago one of the great remedies for almost anything that ailed you was to have a vein opened and a quantity of blood withdrawn. This operation ordinarily took place on the arm, and it was quite a common sight to note people coming out of a barber's shop with the arm bound up in a bloody bandage. So when a new barber opened his shop and wanted to advertise his business he put out a sign showing the white bandage with touches of red here and there. No longer do barbers bleed patients (professionally), yet the old sign remains—only, the red blots have become refined into stripes; the ground is still white. The addition of a stripe of blue is a very recent variation, prompted by the colors of our flag.

Next to the barber shop we often find a drug store; in the show-windows there are probably odd-shaped, big-bellied bottles containing liquids of many hues— red and green and yellow and purple. These are also

81

business signs descended to us from the old days when nobody could paint a picture that would look like the words "chemist," or "pharmacy." The druggist kept his elixirs and extracts in full view; everybody knew that foreign-looking flagons and urns full of strange-tinted fluids were found only in the druggists' shops. Therefore today the store that receives 90 per cent of its income from chewing gum, and writing paper, and candy, and fountain pens, and soda water, and grease-spot removers, and hairbrushes, and only 10 per cent of its revenue from prescriptions, still hangs out the jars of colored water—likely as not above an array of cigars.

Yes, the druggist sells cigars, and we have special cigar stores, too. In front of these, until maybe twenty-five years ago, it was a trade habit to set on the sidewalk a wooden Indian, almost life size, holding in his hand a bundle of cigars. Tobacco, of course, is an American plant and was unknown to Europe until after the discovery of the New World. The shops in London, where tobacco was first sold in Europe, advertised that they stocked the fragrant weed by the display of the wooden Indian. That was quite natural. Then we Americans borrowed from London the Indian that London had borrowed from us.

WHY MEN LIKE BRIGHT TIES

B ECAUSE women decide some things slowly.
Back in the old——

(Indignant Reader: "Hey, wait a minute! Men like bright neckties why? Because women decide slo—what's that got to do with it?")

Back in the old days, several thousand years ago, as I was about to tell you when you interrupted me, man was the more beautiful of the two sexes. He——

(Indignant Reader: "Who—man? Man the more beautiful? Man? Well, of all the—say, if you're going to talk about neckties why don't you talk about them? What have slow decisions to do with neckties? And as for man being beautiful—ho, that's good, that is! Now, are you going to talk about bright ties or not?")

As I was saying, man was the more beautiful of the sexes. That isn't so strange. When we examine the brute creation we find that the male among them is often ornamented and attractive far in excess of the female. Thus the peacock is among the most gorgeous of birds but his mate is truly drab and colorless. The common barnyard rooster has a brilliant red comb, quite large and ornate; his neck is clothed with long silky feathers; his high-arched tail forms a most artistic crescent; yet his modest wife is certainly the reverse, with her stingy little trace of a comb, her stiff short tail and her dull plumage.

The lion and the lioness, as cubs, are so alike in appearance that it is difficult to distinguish between them. But as they grow older the male sprouts a thick outstanding mane. Shave that off, and he would look for all the world like his wife; but with that bushy fringe framing his stern face he wears an air of majesty that prompted our fathers to call him the king of beasts; though others—the elephant, at least—can whip him in fair fight.

Not all the males of animals outshine their demure spouses. But where one sex is the more handsome it is almost without exception the male. So if we find among human beings that the man displays charms denied to his females we need not feel cause for great surprise. And man has several such points. His shoulders and limbs are broader and stouter, as with the lion. His voice is deeper and louder, as with the lion. And his beard, left to grow as Nature designed it, surrounds his face and breast with a mane which astonishingly increases his apparent bulk, as with the lion. And, again like the lion, when his supper isn't ready on time——!

We Americans do not consider our beards very ornamental, so we shave them off every morning. But this

84

was not always the case with mankind. On the carvings which our antiquarians dig up from time to time we see depicted Assyrian nobles, with their beards painstakingly curled—and perhaps they were oiled and scented as well. The Mohammedan, when he wishes to be unmistakably emphatic, swears by the beard of the Prophet. The ancient Jews were forbidden to cut their beards at all. And there are other evidences, well known to scholars, which go far towards proving that hundreds and thousands of years ago our fathers delighted to sport long fluffy beards—and that our mothers admired them.

Under those circumstances—when women gave their smiles to the most ornate suitor—it was a decided advantage for the aspiring lover to have plenty of decoration. If he could flaunt a bigger and fancier beard than his rival that was unquestionably in his favor. But the rival didn't usually give up at the first trial; no, if the girl was worth winning she was worth scheming for. So he ran back to a place near the swimming hole where he remembered seeing some nice red earth, and he daubed himself liberally with that. He came back to the contest glowing like a tomato. The maiden took one glance and her heart stirred within her.

Ugh! Heavy-Beard noted that approving glance and regretted that he had left his club at home. He, too, had seen that red earth; and after kalsomining himself with some of that he picked up two blood-colored feathers that a cardinal bird had dropped, added a green streamer which had belonged to a parrot until the original owner lost it in a fight over a lady-parrot, and—returning with a strut like a turkey-gobbler's—almost put the lady's eye out with his splendor.

The show-off instinct was at work.

Short-Beard retaliated, as best he could with the materials at hand. The maiden inclined first one way, then the other—color and ornament causing her to hesitate, to vacillate, to delay her decision most tantalizingly. And so, during long centuries, man kept inventing new ways to make himself irresistible, and conspicuous, and kaleidoscopic; every novel and outrageous color-combination, added to strings of opalescent shells and other absurdities, giving his lady love an incentive to make up her mind finally and choose him.

Then came civilization and work. Man had other things to think about now. He began to accumulate property—a skin tent, and sheep, and blankets of hides stripped from the victims of his bow and spear. He didn't woo his wives any more; he bought them from their fathers. Daughters began to loom up as assets—if they were able to attract husbands. And the unsought female had to stand the jeers of her peers and the sneers of her parents. But woman had learned a lesson. Leave it to her! She knew now where the red earth lay. She, too, could collect gaudy shells and feathers. So it

86

Why Men Like Bright Ties

became her turn to improve on Nature's art. And did she? She did.

Since that day woman has enjoyed an almost exclusive monopoly of the self-decoration business. Bird-feathers are now for her; animal-furs are for her; the red-tinted skin powders are for her; the glittering stones—the diamond, ruby, emerald—are for her; the silkworm gives up his gleaming strands almost entirely to her; gold is beaten into rings and bracelets—for her. Man discovered work but woman discovered how to work him. Or maybe woman discovered work and sicced him on to it.

Anyway, there still lingers, deep down in the heart of man, a stirring unconscious memory of the days when his ancestors Easter-egged themselves with reds and greens and yellows. As the fat and romping puppy growls unremembered recollections of the battles that his snarling fathers fought, so man of today yearns hungrily to array himself as did his ancestors in scandalous scarlets, and yelping yellows, and violent violets to bedazzle the eye and melt the heart of the reluctant damosel. He doesn't dare to wear them all over, so he wears them in his ties.

"Ah," you object, "but not a man of good taste, surely."

Ask that of your haberdasher, and hear him sigh. "Yes," he'll admit dismally; "it's a fact. When the necktie salesmen come around here they show me some

87

rich aristocratic quiet patterns that are the height of elegance. Just the kind of ties that you and I would wear—refined, sober, genteel. I admire them—oh, man, how I admire them! But I don't buy. Not me. I buy what'll sell—the patterns that ninety-nine men out of ninety-eight want—screaming scarlets, gangrenous greens, blustering blues. The only time we sell real gentlemen's patterns is in December; the women buy 'em for Christmas."

So you see, if our great-grandmothers, seventy-seven times removed, had made up their minds more quickly whether they were going to marry Heavy-Beard or Short-Beard you and I might be wearing neckties of solid dark gray. But we're not. Mine is striped—rose, and red, and magenta, and blue, and black and green. How's yours?

WHY WE BELIEVE HERO TALES

"FATHER," answered little George Washington as he faced his parent manfully, "father, I cannot tell a lie. With my little hatchet I chopped down the cherry tree." And in all his life he never told a fib.

Demosthenes stuttered fearfully as a boy. He determined to become a great orator. So he filled his mouth with pebbles at the seashore and declaimed against the boom and roar of the breaking waves, becoming the most powerful and moving public speaker who has ever lived.

Paul Revere made his midnight ride through scores of towns and villages, awakening the Colonists and warning of the approach of the British. As a result the whole countryside was up in arms to greet the redcoats. Unless Revere had ridden those many, many miles for hour after hour what great disaster would have happened to the Americans!

Before we quote any more wonderful exploits of our school-day heroes let us do a little examining. Have you ever tried to chop down a growing cherry tree? If you have, you know that it is one tough job. The wood is stringy and hard. It seems to have a demoniac power to blunt the ax. A living cherry tree four inches in diameter—and this would be a comparatively young one—is able to furnish an inexpert woodsman all the physical entertainment that he wants for the better part of an hour. After the operation the ax-wielder will be ready to welcome a good long rest, even if his implement was sharp and keen. A little boy with a soft-iron blunt-edged toy hatchet would be a wonder if he could chop down even a cherry sapling. The most he could probably do would be to skin off some of the bark. Besides, even though little Georgie did admit that he had wrought the damage to the tree, nobody ever seems to mention that his veracity is well offset by the fact that he wantonly hacked up a cherished part of his dad's orchard. If it was heroism to tell the truth, was it heroism to commit an act of vandalism? Little boys certainly do go around smashing up things; no doubt about that. But they also maintain a discreet and unbroken silence regarding their exploits in that direction. The story was probably invented to teach children that it is noble not to lie.

Then as to Demosthenes and his stuttering. If a mouthful of pebbles really helps to remedy that misfortune of speech, why don't our doctors recommend it? It isn't that the medicos have a better method of treatment, for they admit that stammering is one ailment that baffles their skill. A few psychologists—notably the psychoanalysts—claim to have discovered the cause

90

and to effect frequent cures, but even they do not pre-scribe the pebble practice. Again, the speeches of Demosthenes have come down to us in print; we read them with delight; they convince us and arouse our emotions just as they did with the Athenians two thou-sand years ago. So it was not the way in which Demos-thenes made his delivery which gained him his great ability to sway the minds of men—it was the thoughts he laid before them. It wasn't how he said it but what he said. He moved his hearers with brain-power. And of course no amount of pebble-exercise would supply brain-power.

And Paul Revere. Last summer I had to spend a day in Boston and in the afternoon I took the rubber-neck bus to visit the surrounding historical spots. In a bare field just a few miles outside of the city there is erected a marker to commemorate the place where Paul Revere was captured by the British. His famous ride didn't extend for more than eight or ten miles out of Boston's city limits, as I recall it now—perhaps not so much as that—and most of it was past farms where there wouldn't be more than one house to the quarter mile on the average. Paul made a good try and deserves full credit for the attempt. But the bare fact is that he was made a prisoner probably within less than an hour after he up-saddled and started out.

Will those facts make any difference in the reception that is given to the tales about Washington and Demosthenes and Revere? Not the least. We, as a nation, have made up our minds that certain anecdotes about great men are true, and all the dry contradictions that meddling busybodies may dig up will not change our acceptance of the traditions one whit. There is something about mankind which makes us gild our heroes with sublime perfection and we refuse to see a flaw in them even if it is pointed out to us. Once a false idea gains currency there is no use in trying to correct it.

That Paul Revere belief is largely due to Longfellow. He wrote an excellent poem about the incident, not troubling himself to adhere too closely to bothersome facts. The poem gained wide circulation, met with warm approval and implanted a misrepresentation that will endure as long as people take pride in American history. Longfellow issued another misstatement that will live longer than anybody who reads this book; it was published under the title, "The Wreck of the *Hesperus.*" That is truly a soul-stirring work; its vivid descriptions of the ocean tempest, its pathetic picture of the bodies of women and children being swept away and washed ashore, its touching scenes among the survivors bring a lump to the throat. As a poem it is superb. As history it embodies one trifling fault—the *Hesperus* wasn't out in the tempest at all; it was lying safely in the harbor all the while and nothing happened to it or to anyone aboard. Longfellow mixed his data, his publishers failed to verify his facts, and so you and

Why We Believe Hero Tales

I have to live in a world which will believe in spite of everything that the *Hesperus* did go down in that terrible night. The poem is so beautiful that the *Hesperus* should have gone down to justify it; and people believe what they want to believe.

Just as we attribute the most incredible virtues to our heroes so do we imbibe eagerly the grossest slanders about our enemies. During the early centuries after Christ the followers of Jesus were accused by their enemies of murdering the children of non-Christians to secure the blood for use in their rituals. Justin Martyr in his Second Apology vigorously defends his coreligionists against this charge. So firmly fixed became the belief that Octavius, Minucius Felix, Tertullian, Origen and other Church Fathers found it necessary indignantly to repudiate the atrocious libel that the Eucharist' involved human sacrifice.

Finally the Christians succeeded in absolving themselves of any possible guilt but the idea survived and had to be fixed on somebody; so it began to be laid at the door of the Jews. And the power of a firmly-rooted belief is so robust that although the Christians began to defend themselves against this libel as early as 150 A. D. it was only a year or so ago—nearly 2,100 years later—that a Jewish family was wiped out in a Russian village because a Christian child was missing— and of course the Jews had killed him to use his blood in their religious observances. Later the child turned

93

up, but that didn't help the victims. A similar charge was reported by the newspapers from Massena, N. Y., in October, 1928, though no lives were imperiled. So the belief still persists in other countries besides Russia. Christian scholars and ecclesiastics have repeatedly declared that scandal untrue. Many of the Popes have issued bulls exonerating the Jews. Have such authoritative denials made any difference to those who chose to believe the charges?

They have not. Everywhere mankind tends to believe that its heroes are entirely good and its enemies entirely bad. The popular belief never says of a prominent man, "He has some excellent virtues and also some human faults." No—he is a hero and hence without any bad, or else an enemy and hence without any good.

When Charles Darwin published his "Descent of Man" the theory outlined therein met with the anguished disapproval of many religious people. The belief gained ground that Darwin was an atheist; no one seems to have believed it worth while to remember that in his third chapter of that same volume Darwin wrote, "The question is of course wholly distinct from that higher one, whether there exists a Creator and Ruler of the universe; and this has been answered in the affirmative by some of the highest intellects that have ever existed," and that in his "Origin of Species" Darwin stated his belief in the Deity. Also the commonly accepted idea is that Darwin claimed that men

94

descended from monkeys. What he really sought to prove was that men and monkeys have a common physical ancestor somewhere far back in the animal kingdom. For example, to say that you and I have a common ancestor in Adam does not at all indicate that you are descended from me, or I from you. Yet the belief persists that the Darwinian theory is that men descended from monkeys, and that Darwin was an atheist. Whether his theory be right or wrong, it is undeniable that many people have a mistaken conception of Darwin's views. And that misconception will continue, now that it has fastened a firm grip on the popular imagination.

You can have fun watching this human tendency in operation. Ask a friend about somebody whom he meets in his daily life; he will admit readily that the other chap has some good points and some weaknesses; now ask the same man about the President or the Governor. If he is an adherent of the official this friend of yours will stoutly maintain that never was there such a perfect Governor or President; but if he belongs to the other political party he will paint the same official as black as Satan.

Our heroes are almost angels in their perfection; our enemies are rank devils. The reason is, of course, that men seek leaders to follow, just as our forefathers gave their allegiance to a tribal chief or king. They will not follow anything less than an ideal; hence the accepted

95

leader is idealized; he is rated as complete perfection. But whatever opposes complete perfection is naturally complete imperfection; so our enemies, opposing our leaders who are all right, promptly prove themselves all wrong.

Without this feeling deeply implanted in the breasts of mankind none of the early tribes could ever have functioned as a group; it would have been merely a band of independently acting individuals, doomed to fall an early prey to better unified tribes which did obey a leader. Without this hero-worship our ancestors could never have developed the civilization which is ours. Their chieftains were god-like in their perfection; so we, too, find in ourselves the impulse to glorify into flawlessness the leaders whom we follow.

Therefore George Washington *did* chop down the cherry tree and he *did* tell the truth about it. Paul Revere *did* ride the country for leagues and leagues and warn all the people. But Benedict Arnold! Obviously, to be capable of winning the implicit confidence of our great Washington, he must really have had some excellent virtues; but he finally turned traitor—and did you ever hear even one word in his favor? You never will.

WHY WE CUT OUR HAIR

IT was the year 480 B. C.

Leonidas, King of Sparta, with 7,000 men, lay encamped at the Pass of Thermopylæ. On the other side of the mountains was approaching the huge army of the Persians, reported by wide-eyed fleeing refugees to number a million and a half—fifteen hundred thousand of the victors who, under their King Xerxes, had swept across Asia and Europe, conquering every nation that they found in their path.

For three years had Xerxes, at the command of his dead father, prepared for this revenge on Greece. Bridges had to be built across the Hellespont—and enormous storehouses of food and equipment for his savage killers along the route. But now he was on the way—nay, almost here.

A million and a half well-armed veterans coming straight to this spot! And only 7,000 Greeks to oppose them. Odds of 200 to 1. There was no hope that the little band could live longer than the day or two that would be required for the Persians to come up to the Pass; in fact, the Greek authorities had sent this handful to Thermopylæ for the open purpose of gaining time while their army could be mobilized. The instructions to Leonidas were, "Hold them as long as you can." It was certain death. The oracle had said that Sparta would be saved by the sacrifice of one of its kings. Not one of those Spartans was ever to see his home or family again. Yet here they waited calmly for death to come. We must admit that they were men.

And, during this awful period until the Persian hordes should reach the Pass, what did these devoted Spartan warriors do to while away the time? They sat in the sun and combed their long hair which they prized so highly. They were on their way to eternity but they were going there looking their best.

In the camp of the Persians the King and the nobles also set great store by the length of their hair. They curled it, and frizzled it, and perfumed it; and quite a few of the great men of the kingdom added false locks to their own, so esteemed were swinging ringlets. It was no sign of effeminacy that these soldiers treasured their long hair; it was only the custom in those days.

Some years before Thermopylæ the Persians had conquered Egypt, and here they encountered a diametrically opposed fashion. The Egyptian men all shaved the head completely. Possibly this was due to the heat with which the Egypt is burdened throughout the year; or—and this is not impossible—since the Egyptians truly considered their rulers to be gods the courtiers

Why We Cut Our Hair

may have shaved their pates in deference to the appearance of some aging Pharaoh who grew bald. When King George of England had his trouser-creases pressed on the sides a few years ago, we must remember, some men in New York actually appeared in public with their creases on the side of the pants, too. And the mummies of bald-headed Pharaohs have been found.

This latter explanation is probably the true one, for the Egyptians let their hair and beard grow only in time of mourning; and this would indicate that the shaving was recognized as a gratifying style, hence unsuitable to a period of humility and affliction. Yet their children of both sexes had the hair shaved from the head, quite likely on account of the heat or vermin. The women, however—clever charmers that they have always been!—wore theirs long and plaited.

Among some of those ancient peoples married women were distinguished from their single sisters by special ways of dressing the hair; and on the opposite side of the world, in China and Japan, we find the same custom existing today, as it has for centuries.

Among the visitors to the shaved Egyptians was Alexander the Great. Whether he first conceived the idea among them is not definitely known, but he did afterwards order his soldiers to shave off the beard, that their adversaries might not use it as a handle while chopping off their heads in battle. Alexander, of course, created an enormous stir in the old times, and we learn from coins which he caused to be struck bearing his image that he himself was smooth-shaven. So in those days it came to be the fashion for military men to shave the face clean. And, next to the priestly class, the military caste has always been held in highest esteem by nations of the past.

But the emperor or king would be numbered among the fighting class, too, and would be shaven. The courtiers would imitate the sovereign; hence we are not surprised to discover that in ancient Rome Julius Cæsar wore no beard, nor did any except a very few of the notables who have come down to us in the history of that period. Cæsar was bald, as were some of his predecessors and successors; and once more we find that the style under bald-headed rulers was for other men to cut their hair short. The Roman matrons, however, added great quantities of false hair to their own, and to dye the locks became quite common among them.

Then came Christianity. Paul regarded it as a shame for a man to have long hair. The clergy exemplified his teachings by cutting their hair short or even shaving their heads. And we are all familiar with pictures of tonsured monks of the Middle Ages who shaved a circle on the pate.

Nevertheless, little by little, men began letting their hair grow, at least down to shoulder-length. The Knights of the Round Table wore theirs so; as did a number of nobles and monarchs who lived after King

Why We Cut Our Hair

Arthur. But it was in the time of Louis XIII of France that hair-dressing rose to almost a mania. Men wore huge white wigs from which depended curls reaching almost to the elbows. And the women—! They had their charming natural strands bepowdered and augmented enormously; fashions in hair-dressing went to greater and greater lengths until the *friseurs* actually constructed imitations of ships in full sail atop their customers' heads; a style that lifted its tip only eight or nine inches above the scalp being considered conservative.

Later, under Louis XV, Madame de Pompadour set a fashion which to a large degree modified the absurd extremes that had prevailed. This was in 1745.

Even yet we see an occasional pompadour.

Fifty years later, in 1795, the American Colonies were subjected to a tax on hair-powder. Previously, however, the influence of the Puritans had made itself felt. Ornate hair-dressing among men, which had begun to wear itself out in this country, soon succumbed to the united attacks of the tax-collector on one hand and the bluestockings on the other.

For a number of years, too, there had been bad blood between England and France. So when it became fashionable for Frenchmen to appear shaved and elaborately bewigged and perfumed, the English dandies decided that it was manly to wear beards and simple wigs or even no wigs at all. Thus in America and in

101

Why We Do It

England different forces combined to introduce again the wearing of short hair among men.

A portrait gallery of our Presidents clearly traces subsequent developments. Washington and Adams and Jefferson wore carefully dressed hair and smooth faces. Lincoln and Grant and Harrison inherited the style of short hair and beards. Our Southern Colonels affected mustaches and goatees. And then came a purely modern development—advertising in combination with the safety razor—and now we have been thoroughly sold as a nation on the daily shave.

We believe sincerely that the custom of wearing short hair will remain constant among men, but it is well not to feel too sure. Who would have predicted in 1915 that women all over the world were going to adopt the bob? If history be a safe guide we may expect to see them wearing long hair again, with wigs filling in the transition period. Does some one contend that men are not so silly as to burden themselves with long hair? Pooh! What is sillier than constricting the neck with a high tight collar? Yet we do that. Because other men do it, of course; but suppose they all took to wearing their hair long again—then what?

WHY WE GROW ANGRY

FOR the same reason that we like candy.

What? Say that again.

We grow angry for the same reason that we like candy.

"Ho, that's wrong," taunts a quick-witted friend; "we get angry because things happen that we don't like."

Well, I'm growing older every day; I don't like that but certainly I don't wax angry over it. You don't like the idea of paying for life-insurance year after year and not collecting any of it; and still less do you like to think of the time when it will be collected; yet you don't flare up and show temper. But now let a stranger in the street-car step on your foot purposely; or let the waiter in a restaurant walk up and take away your food before you have well begun to eat it, and what happens? You feel your muscles stiffen, your heart pumps faster, and you are ready to fight.

So our friend was only half right. Really, what makes us angry is some occurrence that we do not like—and which we believe we might remedy or avenge by our personal effort. We may complain about the

103

cold winter, but we know there is nothing we can do about it, so we never think of becoming irate. But if our host ejects us from his warm house into the cold dark night and tells us never to come back again we dare him to come outside and fight like a man. It isn't the cold that enrages us—it is the reparable offense.

We are so accustomed to being angry before we fight that it never occurs to us to wonder why we can't fight without having to lose our temper first. And when somebody tells us that we lose our temper for the same reason that we like candy we—I won't say it, but we think it just the same, don't we?

But here are the facts. We like candy because it is nearly pure sugar. And sugar is not only all food but it is absorbed into the body and releases its energy to our muscles quicker than anything else that we eat. That is why children crave sweets; they get from sugar such a quick supply of the power that they are constantly expending.

And now Dr. Hackebusch discovers that both fear and anger cause our glands to pour a stream of sugar into the blood. In his laboratory he tested the blood of human subjects in his experiments and found a tiny quantity of grape sugar usually present. Then he aroused either fear or anger, again withdrawing a blood sample for a sugar test. In every case he was able to analyze out a far greater proportion of grape sugar.

Now, when we fight from anger or when we run from

fear we spend energy quite rapidly. And Dr. Hacke-busch concluded that the body supplies this extra amount of sugar to the blood in anticipation of the violent motion that is expected as a result of the violent emotion. The easily-absorbed sugar is poured into the blood stream to give the fast-working muscles the added food and energy that they are going to require. Fear and anger are Nature's ways of preparing us for fight or flight.

Here we may find the explanation of a widespread phenomenon. It has often been remarked that the small and the weak are quicker to display irritability than are the big and strong. When the powerful man meets ordinary situations calmly it may well be that he feels within himself sufficient force to overcome them. A less favored individual, confronted with the same obstacles, instinctively realizes that they are greater than his habitual effort can subdue. To meet them successfully will require a severe struggle on his part. If his glands release sugar freely his muscles and mind will respond to the stimulus and enable him to cope with the diffi-culty more easily. So a hot temper really serves the slender five-footer somewhat as an equalizer between himself and his bulky six-foot antagonist. Behind the scenes in a vaudeville show I once heard a three-foot dwarf swearing dreadfully at a seven-foot giant who could have crushed him with one hand—and the giant yawned in tolerant unconcern.

105

Why We Do It

As a result of this new knowledge we might have to change some of our common expressions. We used to say that a placid person who did not quickly show anger was sweet-tempered. But now we learn that a man of sour disposition is sweeter. His body contains more free sugar. To a cannibal he might actually taste like dessert. Perhaps we may one of these days be saying, "Jim is wonderfully sweet-tempered; he gets angry at everything."

WHY WE ENJOY OYSTERS

"ALL right," rejoined my friend in the dining car with me; "if you don't think the first man who ever ate an oyster was a hero you wait until we arrive in Montreal. I'll take you to a French restaurant and let's see you eat a snail."

That is a challenge which most of us would hesitate to accept. A strange gentleman at the same table relieved me from an embarrassing situation when he smiled. "I have eaten snails," he volunteered. "They're good—mighty good."

When you get right down to it, just what is the difference between snails and oysters as dietary delicacies? Just habit. Here in America we are accustomed to oysters and clams. We relish them immensely. Yet if we had never seen these bivalves, if we had grown up among people who customarily ate snails, no doubt we should find snails very acceptable indeed.

In Mexico once I had an amusing illustration of how strongly habit regulates our choice of food. It was up in the mountains of the mining district, and I had taken

107

Why We Do It

a Kickapoo Indian along with me as guide during a prospecting trip. When we sat down to eat our first meal he drew out of his saddlebags some cooked meat from which he brushed with his hand bits of leaves and other refuse picked up from the interior of the leather pocket. The meat was old—too old. Its odor and appearance were so repulsive to me that I lost my desire for lunch. Instead I walked away for a bit of fresh air.

That night when we camped I made it a point to wait until he had selected a place to finish his meat before I sat down to eat. Moving away to some distance I opened a can of lambs' tongues and a package of soda crackers. In a few moments the Indian arose and came over to say something to me. When he glimpsed my supper he gazed at it for a while with a puzzled expression. Then he picked up the paper napkin on which I had laid the tongues. The soft meat crushed in his grasp, the cold jellied sauce quivered. With one horrified glance at me, and seeing that I was eating this strange food, the Kickapoo dropped what he held, wiped his hand quickly on the mesquite grass with a grunt of disgust and suffered severely from nausea.

So there is truth as well as philosophy in the old saw which declares that what is one man's meat is another man's poison.

During the Great War the people of America were

108

urged to ship food overseas to help feed our allies. We were told quite bluntly that "Food will win the war." So we put ourselves on rations and shipped hundreds of tons of good corn across the seas to England and France and starving Belgium. And what happened?

Corn was a new food to those men and women. They had never eaten it before. And they refused to eat it then. Piteous indeed were the appeals which came to us to send food to the hungry populations. But corn was not food, to them, and they refused to touch it. So we ate the corn and sent them our wheat.

They did eat horse flesh. To many Belgians and Germans the meat of horses had been a customary dish for many generations. During the height of the conflict, when the submarine blockade was proving most effective, the family that could sit down to a dinner of horse steak was considered lucky indeed. And before we condemn our friends across the water for rejecting our corn let us think what we would have said had we begged them for meat and received several boatloads of horse meat in response to our prayer. Can you imagine the wail that would have gone up?

The part that habit plays in affecting our views of desirable food is clearly displayed within the limits of one racial group. The orthodox Jewish people, who have been trained from childhood to consider pork as forbidden, manifest a lively disgust at the thought of consuming the meat of hogs, as I have reason to believe

109

from experiences which have occurred in my presence. Yet Jewish citizens of the "reformed" faith find pork quite as toothsome as does anyone else. It cannot be that there is any anatomical difference in the two groups to account for this, and the meat in either case is exactly the same. The only reason why some like pork and some physically abhor it is the effect of training and habit.

In my own household there is a maid whom we have brought to New York from Mexico in order that our children may learn to speak Spanish. She is docile and obedient in all things, but when I eat a certain kind of cheese made here in America she is always excused from serving it. In fact, she is permitted to retire to her own part of the house, as the odor makes her ill. Thousands of Americans besides myself eat this cheese and like it; it is served everywhere in the best of clubs. Hence it cannot be so very deadly. Yet when I mention to this maid that in her own Mexico I have seen peddlers on the street selling strips of goatskin the size of a man's hand, which had been cleaned of hair and fried; and that I have seen others selling little paper peanut sacks filled with fried locusts, she maintains stoutly that these are not necessarily repulsive—at least, they are not even to be compared with a cheese such as I eat.

The Mexican peon enjoys his fried locusts; I enjoy my Liederkranz; neither of us would exchange with

110

the other; both are happy. Could anyone desire more?
What a grand world it is!

Some years ago at Coney Island one of the exhibits
was a small Igorote settlement, tenanted by semi-wild
savages brought from the Philippine Islands. Time and
again I have seen Americans turn away in horror when
one of these barbarians slit the throat of a dog, dis-
membered the animal and threw the parts into a cal-
dron to cook for dinner. Without in the slightest
manner wishing to advocate dogs as food, may we not
still inquire wherein their flesh differs from other meat?
The only explanation that I receive from laymen is
that the dog is carnivorous and we do not use the flesh
of meat-eaters as food. But fish, turtles and crabs eat
meat, and we pay a good price for them. Chickens
delight in meat when they are lucky enough to have it.
The only apparent explanation is the force of habit.

This feeling of repulsion towards strange food may
even go to the extreme of arousing wholly false beliefs
as to its effect on the health. When my sister visited
Germany once as a little child tomatoes were raised
there only as garden ornaments, the fruit being generally considered poisonous. And the young lady enjoyed quite a bit of notoriety as the little American
girl who could eat "Paradise apples" without being
made sick. The performance in front of an awestruck
crowd, she told me, has more than once yielded her the
marked respect of the onlookers who marveled at her

Why We Do It

astounding ability to withstand the tomato's virulence. She eats them yet, and lives!

When I was a boy my Boston grandmother used to divide a single banana between my brother and myself, bananas being poisonous except in small doses. And more than one thin slice of watermelon at a time was denied us for the same salutary reason. But my brother Frank and I, having been reared in Texas, had no such beliefs; and we calmly waited until the good old lady had gone elsewhere, when we promptly swiped as much more as we could hold.

So when there is next set before us a succulent dish of oysters let us give a kindly thought to the French peasant who is enjoying sweet dreams as a result of the excellent supper of snails which he finished only a few hours before.

WHY WE USE PATRONYMICS

NOT all the nations of the earth have named their children after the family of the father. The Tahitians, as one example, called their children after the maternal side of the house. And a surprising number of tribes have at some time or other been matriarchates—dominated by women. Our own male ancestors, however, were the heads of their respective families. Whatever belonged to the group was understood as belonging to the husband. He owned the dogs and the spears, just as he owned the children and the women.

It is only since the Christian era began, or thereabouts, that family names became general. What was John the Baptist's last name? Or Christ's? They had none. In those days and among most of the people of the earth a man was "the son of" somebody—somebody who was known to both speakers. Thus we read of James, the son of Zebedee; a man in his own town was known in that way to distinguish him from others also named James; if he came from another city his father wouldn't be known in his new place of residence and he would then be best described as James of such-and-such a locality; one famous example is Joseph of Arimathea—he was living in Jerusalem but he had moved there from another town.

That "son of" method of naming has been used by the most varied nations. The Scandinavian plan of tacking "son" on the end of the father's name is daily encountered in such familiar forms as Ericson (the son of Eric), and Johnson, and Olafson, and Christopherson, and Matthewson, and Larson.

The Russians do it. In their language "witz" or "vich" has the same meaning as "son." Thus we have Ivanovich (the son of Ivan), and Rabinovitz, and Nikolaivich, and Mannewitz. The Czar's eldest son was the Czarevich.

Among the Polish people the syllable "ski" serves a similar purpose. We meet a Pole named Pulaski and we know then that one of his ancestors was called Pula. His cousin is Paderewski (son of Patrick), or Levinski, or Pilsudski, or Lorski. But not McClusky.

For the McClusky's originated in Scotland. There MacBeth was the son of Beth, and MacBain the son of Bain, and MacDonald the son of Donald. All the Macs and Mcs are the "sons" of some Scottish ancestor; for among the old Scots Mac meant the same as *ski* or *vich* or *son*.

Across the Channel in Ireland a somewhat similar process took place. James, son of Neill, became shortened into James O'Neill. Thus the O'Gilvies and the

114

Why We Use Patronymics

O'Connells and the O'Gradys and the O'Haras can name one of their forefathers even though they may have preserved no family tree. True, among the Irish, as among the Scots, a man might take his name from his clan. But as the clan was known by its leader there is small real difference.

The Macs, the O's, the -skis and the -viches represent a long descent from some far-off progenitor, but they are quite recent when compared to the traceable parentage of Mr. Cohen and Mr. Levi. In your Bible you read that the tribe of Levi was dedicated to the Lord as His especial servants. A Levite was born into the priestly class. Even the most dissolute and degraded descendant of Levi enjoyed a certain honor which could never be equaled by the most noble son of any of the other eleven tribes. Now, while the Levites were all eligible to the priesthood, and possibly in some manner or other served in offices connected with the Temple, yet the real acting priests were the Levites of a special rank—the *Cohannim*. So Nat Cohen, we know, not only descends in a straight line from Levi, but one of his ancestors was a *Cohan*—a priest of Israel.

Later on, as nobility developed in some of the European countries, the more distant relatives of a famous man found it agreeable to connect themselves with him in public. So we have with us the de Hautevilles, and the de Beers, and the de Laines, hailing originally from

115

Why We Do It

France—the *de* meaning simply "of the family." Thus Hugh d'Arcy is Hugh of the family of (the famous) Arcy. Joan of Arc in her home town was Jeanne d'Arc —Joan of the Bow. Perhaps one of her forebears had been a skilled archery shot. Later Joan was ennobled, you know, and some of the D'Arcys claim to descend from her brothers.

In Germany the same custom attended the "von." Ullrich von Graffhausen was Ullrich, a relative of (the great) Graffhausen outfit. Speck von Sternberg claimed kinship to the aristocratic house of Sternberg. During the Empire days of France the nobles were as jealous of their *de* as the present Germans are of their *von*. No commoner was permitted to use either *de* or *von*. If a fisherman or a cheesemonger now happens to be named Graffhausen his son Ulrich is simply Ulrich Graffhausen.

The nobility received many of their family names from some notable ancestor or perhaps from one of his exploits. But the commoners were often named after their trades. Herman Schmidt's ancestor was a smith in Germany. Adolf Koch's was a chef. Heiny Meister's was an overseer or a foreman. Gustav Zimmerman's was a carpenter.

Our English forefathers received their family names in similar fashion. We know at once what was the trade of some far-back ancestor of the Barbers, the Weavers, the Taylors, the Cutlers.

Why We Use Patronymics

Turning to Holland, we are quite confident that our Vanderbilts had at least one artist in their lineage; for he was Cornelius van der Bilt—Cornelius of the Picture. And the first Mr. Kahn or Kahner was probably a waterman, for a *Kahn* is a boat.

During the days of Napoleon—so my own family legend tells me—the Emperor insisted that all men should bear a family name; no more of this "Jim the son of Pete" stuff was to go. The oldest member of a family was to be given his choice of a patronymic and all his descendants were to bear it too. The head of our crowd, Wolff the son of Daniel, was well along in years, and deaf—and, I suspect, a little stubborn or maybe fat-headed. Anyway, he lined up in front of the judge with the rest of them, and when his turn came the judge said, "Well, Wolff, what do you want to be named?"

"Huh?"

"What do you want to be named?"

"Huh?"

"You've got to have a name, you know. That's the law. What do you want yours to be?"

"Name? Name? I've got one. It's Wolff." So they wrote it that way in the book, and the old gentleman was Wolff Wolff. That's probably hokum, but it's the way I am supposed to have received my family name. Where did yours come from?

117

WHY WE DEFER EYE-GLASSES

W E were sitting in the lady's living room that afternoon. I smoked and listened as she embroidered and talked. The monologue went something like this, "And I said, 'Do you?' and she said, 'I certainly do,' and I said, 'Well, if I were in your place——' Darn it!"

I looked up surprised at the unexpected termination.

The lady had punctured her thumb with the needle, and a drop of red oozed out onto the initial that she was working. While she excused herself to render first aid to the wound I had time to reflect.

Here was a damsel of some thirty summers or so, single and not at all unattractive. Even before the afternoon's chat I had rather guessed that her eyes needed the assistance of lenses; there was something about the perk of her head and the squint around the corners of her eyes that told me so. Because we are old friends I had taken the liberty of asking whether she had ever felt that her eyes grew tired and whether she had ever thought about having them examined.

"Ho, no," was the answer. "Glasses? Nonsense! They're all a habit, anyway. Once you start using

118

them you have to keep it up. Look at you; yours are never off."

Then, because I am no diplomat, I argued. Do you think it made any impression? Do you?

The sober truth, of course, is that the lady, being single, will not wear glasses because she wants to look young and she thinks they would make her look old. In her premise she is unquestionably right; everyone should look as young as possible; a young world is a happy world. But in her conclusion I fear she was sadly mistaken.

I have told you, haven't I, that she squinted up her eyes while she sewed? I have seen her do the same thing while reading. Every time she screws tight the little muscles around her eyes she folds the flesh into creases. These creases, in time, have become permanent. Now they are wrinkles. And they grow wrinklier and wrinklier with each successive squinting of her eyes.

Then another thing. Squinting makes deep lines at other places than around the eyes. Prove this by a little experiment. Squint your eyes. Do you feel your upper lip lift? With your fingers you can feel the flesh next to the wings of the nose sink into deep ridges when you close your eyes forcibly. Those same ridges form when you squint. They, too, in time, grow deeper and deeper, more and more permanent.

Remember that, for a moment, while we consider something else. It is not at all uncommon to see young

119

children wearing glasses nowadays. This is a wise move on the part of parents to aid the eye while it is still young and tender; glasses at an early age may so improve the vision and ease the eye-strain that artificial help will not be needed when the child becomes adult. Even if this happy result is not achieved the glasses certainly almost always do prevent the trouble from becoming worse; they preserve for the child the best vision that his eyes can give. They save him from the misery of headaches, and nervousness, and stomach disorders and the host of other ills which march in the train of poor eyesight. In adults, naturally, these symptoms are far more severe than they are in children. Nearly always, when you see a grown person who is nervous and miserable generally, without any obvious cause, you will be pretty safe if your first guess is, "Eye-strain."

It used to be that only old people wore spectacles. Oculists went on the assumption that young eyes were necessarily good eyes; they know better now. At lunch the other day a scientist told me that more than one-third of all Americans need glasses, and that only one-third of those who need lenses are wearing them.

Think of it! Out of every three people who require spectacles to make their lives happier only one enjoys that benefit; the other two suffer—and wonder why.

During the old days, when only aged people wore glasses, it might have been quite a proper thought that

Why We Defer Eye-Glasses

all who wore glasses were aged. But when we see youngsters of twelve and fourteen using lenses to help their eyesight is there any good reason for believing that glasses are a sign of age?

At all events, well-fitted lens-frames on a smooth, rosy, young-looking face form a much more charming picture than bloodshot eyes staring wearily out from between a network of crows'-feet and wrinkles, don't you think?

But let us grant the argument that glasses make the wearer look old. Then what? The patient still has a choice of two alternatives—he can look old as a result of wearing glasses, or he can look old as a result of eye-strain, crows'-feet and wrinkles. Which does he prefer? For he must choose one, of course.

I wonder whether you will agree with me when I suggest choosing the glasses. It seems to me that they have all the advantage in this contest. Firstly, glasses can be removed, but nobody can remove wrinkles— except the skin-lifters, maybe, and even they wouldn't help in this case, because continued squinting would bring the wrinkles right back again. And we can't go on lifting the skin forever.

Yes, glasses can be removed from time to time, but wrinkles can't. But that isn't the worst of it. Let a man deceive himself as much as he will, let him squint and wrinkle and ridge his skin as much as he likes, the time is coming when his weak vision is going to compel the

121

use of glasses anyway. He may convince himself for a
while that his eyes don't need attention but he can't
convince his eyes of that. They'll strain and tug as
long as they can—and then when they do go they'll
quite likely need strong lenses before them continuously. But by that time the wearer will have the glasses,
and the wrinkles, and the crows'-feet, and the cheek-
valleys all at once. That's hardly a picture of youth,
is it?

So sooner or later the glasses are coming, if your
eyes need them. If they come soon they will help to
keep your skin smooth and fresh-looking. If you hold
them off until later, every day that passes will tool
the telltale age-marks a little deeper into the skin. In
other words, you may have glasses with a youthful face
or glasses with a wrinkle-marked face. So even if spectacles do make you look older, you'll look younger if
you wear them now than if you wait even a year or
perhaps only six months.

In this wise and profound fashion did I discourse
with the damsel who is single and not unattractive. It
was the most crushing and unanswerable argument in
favor of saving the eyes and preserving one's youthful
appearance that I ever heard in my life. It was delivered in a manner that left but one possible decision.
I waited to hear what the damsel had to say.

She said, "Will you have lemonade or a nice hot cup
of tea?"

122

WHY WE FEAR THIRTEEN

A S an introduction to this chapter you are to make an experiment. In a group of friends suggest a new game. You will distribute a slip of paper and a pencil to each one present. When all are ready ask them to write down any number less than ten—any number at all—the first that pops into their heads. When they have done this and folded up their papers, announce that you will have somebody else collect the papers, tabulate the numbers and reveal to all present except yourself how many wrote 1, how many listed 2, and so on. Then, when everybody but you knows the result you agree to call out the one number which appeared the oftenest. Your friends will greet this offer with incredulity, which will change to surprise when you, without hesitation, select the correct number.

They will clamor to know how you did it. And the trick lies in the fact that you didn't do it at all—they did. You knew before the game even started just which number most of them would choose. The greater the crowd the more certain you may feel that the larger share of them under such a test will write just one number every time. That number is seven.

Why We Do It

I haven't the faintest idea why it is that seven seems
to be the favorite; so far as I can learn nobody knows.
There appears to be some quirk of the human mind
which makes it prefer seven above all the other numbers below ten, but the cause for this is obscure. Nevertheless the number seven has for ages exercised its spell
over the mental operations of our ancestors.

Moses fashioned for the Temple a seven-branched
candlestick. The ancient Greeks said that they saw in
the Pleiades seven stars, though some of us can see
only six or five and others eight or nine. The week has
seven days; and after the Creation it was the seventh
day on which God rested. Jacob labored seven years for
Rachel; discovering that her father, Laban, had sub-
stituted her sister Leah in Rachel's place Jacob labored
yet seven more years to secure his beloved to wife. The
son who succeeded Aaron was to put on his father's
robes seven days; Leviticus commands that the blood
of the offering shall seven times be sprinkled towards
the mercy seat; Jacob bowed himself before his brother
Esau seven times; and throughout the Bible we have
such references as in the last verse of the first chapter
of the Revelation: "The mystery of the seven stars
which thou sawest in my right hand, and the seven
golden candlesticks. . . ."

Three is another number which has captivated the
mind, perhaps through its Biblical and other associa-
tions. The friends who visited Job were three. The

124

Why We Fear Thirteen

Wise Men of the East who came to worship the infant Christ were three. We have the Holy Trinity. Three has had no especial significance attached to it in popular belief; though seven, from its remarkable repetition in the Bible, for many centuries was considered to be a lucky number.

Quite opposed to this is the fatality inseparably fixed in some minds in connection with the number thirteen. This arose nearly two thousand years ago as a consequence of an assemblage of thirteen men which immediately preceded the greatest moment in Christian history—the Last Supper, to which Jesus sat down with his twelve disciples. Thirteen represented the number of those partaking; this was on Thursday night and on the next day occurred the Crucifixion. To this day there are hundreds of people who firmly refuse to sit at table with twelve others, confident that if they do one of the company will shortly die.

Just why it is but one who will suffer death is difficult to fathom, for of the thirteen who sat at meat in Jerusalem twenty centuries ago two passed out of this life at almost the same time—Christ and Judas. It would appear reasonable, therefore, to expect that of thirteen diners two would die, but the popular notion predicts this fate for only one—doubtless because Judas, the betrayer, is not of sufficient importance to influence the welfare of others.

We saw a moment ago that the Last Supper occurred

on Thursday. The Crucifixion, that terrible tragedy of Christendom, took place on Friday—a day forever memorable as timing the greatest misfortune conceivable to the followers of the Nazarene. Friday has borne that stigma thenceforth through the ages, and all of us know sensible and practical people who manage not to start any important undertaking on that day. In support of their belief they remind us that one of the greatest financial disasters in American history began on a day known as "Black Friday." And in some States Friday is the customary day for the commission of legal executions. The choice is based on Friday's reputation as a day of catastrophe, and has no connection whatever with the execution which was perpetrated under Pontius Pilate.

During past ages mankind has consistently attributed good or bad luck to times or objects or the most varied ideas, sometimes for reasons that are capricious in the extreme, sometimes for a cause not at all obvious but which is quite understandable when explained. To take an example, consider the horseshoe. To find one of these presages good fortune. Why? It promises neither good luck nor bad luck to run across a bridle, or a rein, or a trace, or a bit. Why, then, is he fortunate indeed who comes upon a horseshoe in his path? A few paragraphs back we learned that seven, on account of its frequency in Biblical numerology, has always borne a reputation for luck. Did you ever count

126

the nail-holes in a horseshoe? There are—how many? Yes, you guessed it the first time. Seven. Hence the luck.

Does a found horseshoe convey enough good luck to offset the bad luck which will follow breaking a mirror? Personally I think not, and here's an anecdote which will tell you why.

When I was a boy the correct procedure on finding a horseshoe was to spit on it and throw it over the left shoulder, not looking to see where it fell. All three of those notions—the magic efficacy of human saliva, the choice of the left shoulder and refraining from learning the object's final resting place—all have a long and respectable ancestry which we have no time to examine now. What reminded me of it was the time Deddie Herff found a horseshoe, carried out the customary and prescribed rites and—broke a mirror with it! The mirror happened to be hanging in his own home; and Deddie's mother, hearing the crash, promptly investigated. The result was of such a nature as to convince me that it is far worse luck to break a mirror than it is good luck to find a horseshoe. I haven't asked Deddie his opinion about this in recent years but I am willing to wager that he still thinks as I do.

What started this broken mirror superstition is the fact that the smooth surface reflects the human body, as we see whenever we use a looking-glass. Our ancestors, being simple people, somehow couldn't disconnect

127

Why We Do It

from each other the real body and its strikingly life-like image. Naturally, shattering the mirror caused the apparent disappearance of the body—and who wants to disappear? That would be hard luck indeed. Another explanation is that years ago, when mirrors were very costly, housemaids were told that breaking such a valuable possession would bring them bad luck —and if the mistress was at all hot-tempered I don't doubt that it did. But as there are traces of the belief dating from the time when mirrors were made of pol-ished metal (and therefore not breakable by careless maids) I am inclined to accept the body-mutilation theory, since the horrible misfortunes consequent on scratching those bronze mirrors were the same as we are threatened with now when we break one of glass; and deep scratches across a plate of metal would dis-figure the reflected body and arouse the most discon-certing and terror-waking presentiments of evil about to overtake the gazer.

Do you like spiders? No? Well, you're making a mistake, I fear. Spiders bring luck. Everybody re-members that when Robert Bruce was hiding from his enemies he crept into a cave, across which a spider immediately stretched her web. His pursuers, finding the cave, were about to search its interior, when one of them pointed out that the web was unbroken and so Bruce could not possibly have crawled in there. They went away and Bruce was saved. So you see you have

128

reason to believe that spiders bring luck—if you happen to be Scotch, that is. Of course, if you are English and your ancestors were among those pursuers you might take a different view. But the spider superstition has a firmer ground than this.

During the sixteenth century, while doughty mariners were seeking a northwest passage to Cathay (the land we know as China), a rescued seaman brought home from the island where he had been cast ashore a stone which was found to contain gold. You can imagine the flurry that ensued. Our old friend Martin Frobisher headed a treasure-hunting expedition, fitting up galleons of hard wood into which he loaded, among other things, gallons of hard drink.

Some people have all the luck! He found the island which the sailor had described, took ashore some food, fools and tools, set the food before himself and the tools before the fools and proceeded to dig—by proxy. Yet, would you believe it, they actually did find gold. The island was infested with an enormous quantity of spiders, and ever since then Martin Frobisher, and the little Frobishers, and the uttermost descendants of Martin Frobisher even unto this day believe that spiders bring luck. Yet so perverse are human beings that I have never seen anybody pick up a spider in his fingers and talk kindly to it. We don't deserve good fortune.

WHY WE NOTCH OUR LAPELS

L AST night a friend of mine exhibited a gold snuff box which has been in his family's possession for more than a century. It was a gift from Napoleon to my friend's great-grandfather. The owner was highly delighted with the idea of its great age. "This is the only thing in our house," he explained, "which has so long a history." But he was mistaken.

At the very time when our host was showing us the snuffbox he was displaying a number of items which trace farther back in time. They were all in the suit that he was wearing. Yet he received the garment from his tailor only a few weeks ago, and you can have a bit of fun puzzling your acquaintances with a question about their clothes that appears to be quite simple to answer, but nearly all of them will slip up on it.

Here it is:

In the left hand lapel of every man's coat is a buttonhole. Ask the wearer its purpose. With a supercilious smile he will inform you that it is placed there to hold a flower. Then ask him why a double-breasted suit has a buttonhole in both lapels. Is it to make room for two flowers—one on each side? While he is deciding how angry he ought to be you can go on with your story.

The truth is that the buttonhole in the lapel is a hangover some four or five hundred years old. Once it had a very definite reason for its existence; it served a useful purpose, as you can evidence with an easy experiment.

Unbutton your coat and turn up the collar all around. If now you will button the coat again you will see that the lapel with the buttonhole falls into just the right position so that, if it had a button to embrace, it would close your coat tightly right up to your chin. You will have what seems to be a "military" stand-up collar such as Columbus, and Sir Isaac Newton, and Napoleon, and Washington, and most of the other heroes pictured in the history books used to wear—and like the men in a brass band have on their uniforms even today.

Thus we arrive at the solution of our mystery. Uniforms, like laws, preserve for us unchanged certain customs of the past. Once, when both the rigid uniforms and the stylish clothing of today were in their infancy, all men wore coats with "military" collars. When a man went out into the cold he buttoned his coat up snugly around his throat. When he came into a warm—or comparatively warm—building he opened the upper button for comfort. If the house happened to be warm indeed, he turned his collar down around

131

his neck because that threw the lapels wide apart, giving him more freedom and air. If he wore a double-breasted suit sometimes he buttoned it from left to right and sometimes from right to left.

Of course, under those circumstances, the buttonhole in the lapel was necessary. Any suit that didn't have it was incomplete. Today our coats don't have a button away up on top on the right-hand side, and so the lapel buttonhole on the left is a grass widower, so to speak—or half of a twin, if you prefer that comparison. The button is gone but its buttonhole remains, faithful throughout the centuries, patiently awaiting a mate which will never return.

Now, when you looked in the mirror a moment ago, did you ask yourself why there is a notch in each lapel? "Huh, every coat has those notches," objects someone. Yes, but why?

Well, turn up your coat collar again. With your finger hold the left lapel where it would stay if the other side of the coat had a button to catch its buttonhole. Do you see how the upper edge of the lapel lies flat on your chest while the short collar-edge stands upright? How else could you attach such a collar? The notch wasn't intentionally designed as a notch, you see—it just happened. Our ancestors, in opening their throat-buttons and turning down the collar, found that where collar joined coat in front there remained quite naturally a right-angled notch.

Why We Notch Our Lapels

Different men, different manners; the style changed and all the red hot sports began to wear their coat collars turned down continuously. Stand-up collars went out of fashion. Only lay-down collars were the mode. The tailors, however, went on cutting coats as they always had, putting on collars that were useless and forming notches which were unnecessary. And so you and I have to wear on our clothes vestiges of a time that has been part of eternity these many hundreds of years.

Let us not smile in derision at those old-timers. We are no stronger of character than were they. We could, of course, remove the collar and lapels from our coats. We could—but we don't dare. What a holy sight for the multitude we should be, arrayed in such manner! That's how our forebears felt about it, no doubt. And, like them, we continue meekly to parade the earth, bearing about our shoulders the relics of a forgotten custom, wasting good cloth in a world which hasn't enough wool to clothe itself without the admixture of cotton or shoddy in much of its outer raiment.

On the cuff of my friend's coat sleeve were three small buttons, set close together. And at the lower end of the sleeve, where the two edges of the cloth tube joined, the seam had been left open for about an inch. In cheap clothes, where every stitch of labor and every bit of material affects the cost, we see as a rule but one button, and the seam of the sleeves is closed down

133

its entire length. But in good clothes, the kind in which
the maker takes a real pride, you will usually find two
to four buttons and the seam is almost always left open
a bit of the way from the bottom. Clothing manufac-
turers will tell you, "That is a mark of fine tailoring.
All good clothes have it." All right, but why?

They don't leave our trousers open at one seam
around the ankle. They don't trim the bottom trouser
edge with little buttons for us, do they? Maybe those
things would be the mark of fine tailoring too, we suggest. Promptly and firmly comes the answer, "Certainly
not." Then why are they an indication of good crafts-
manship when found on the sleeve?

Not one clothing man in a score can tell us. Perhaps he wouldn't if he could, because people who ask
too many questions are likely to be a nuisance. Yet
there is a hoary, hot-blooded ancestry behind those
two apparently trifling and whimsical finishing touches.
And, though we do not stop to realize it, they convey
just a hint of gentle flattery, too.

For back in the gallant days of Bonnie Prince
Charlie every real he-man of any quality at all packed
a sword. Yes, and used it with an indiscriminating and
unrestrained alacrity that reflected more credit on his
courage than on his judgment. A lovable, boastful,
vainglorious, pompous race of swashbucklers—hard
drinkers, hard swearers, hard riders and hard fighters;
ready at any time for a feast, a frolic or a fracas;

Why We Notch Our Lapels

and—if the facts were known—probably often encountering an enemy where they had expected to find an enamorata.

All one to that crowd! A courteously insulting question, a soul-scorching response contemptuously tossed back, and the ready challenge. Hastily was the skintight wrist of the coat unbuttoned, the sleeve and the cascading lace shirt-cuff rolled back to the elbow, given the grave ritualistic salute and—zizz, zizz, zizz!—steel slid over steel, until a cold metal point plunged deep into warm living flesh, and blood gushed forth to testify a victory.

There it is, you see. Because your seven-times-great-grandfather flourished a mean saber he had need for buttons and buttonholes, that he might bare his fighting arm quickly. The long slit which ran up his sleeve from wrist to elbow is narrowed down in our day to a mere rudimentary inch-long open seam, and his string of a dozen buttons shrunken to a bare two or three. Which is perhaps quite as well; because I, for one, would rather blow a police whistle at midnight than participate in a rapier duel in a dark and muddy street. There is less romance in the police whistle, perhaps, but considerably more longevity.

Locomotion in those brave days went afoot—human or equine. If granddad had a long journey to make he stuffed his belongings into his capacious coat pockets before he mounted his nag. Then, to keep from jogging everything into the road, he buttoned down over the pocket-mouth a flap which his tailor had provided. And today you, his descendant of the thirteenth generation, have flaps over your coat pockets, even though you chuck your Gladstone into the rear seat of your limousine and haven't the faintest idea of how one cranks up a saddle-horse or shifts the gears on him from a trot to a lope. Also, because granddad had to sit astride a horse, you have an open vent in the back of your coat to fit over a saddle.

So my friend of last night bore about with him many antiquities which far outnumbered Napoleon's memento in the years of their lineage. There were more than we have spoken about here, but this chapter is long enough already.

WHY WE MOURN IN BLACK

BECAUSE our forefathers believed in ghosts. That is literally true.

Death has always touched mankind with a deep sense of the mysterious. It is so unexplainable. For many years we are acquainted with a man. We know him, as we say. But what is it that we know? His physical appearance, his disposition, his power to do us good or harm. As long as he lives he is to us a promise or a threat; but, in whatever way we think of him, part of the picture is his ability to want to do things and his power to carry out his wishes. Then suddenly one day we see him dead. His appearance is unchanged. Yet no longer does he seem to have the ability to wish nor the power to do things. Something has gone from him. We call it the life. But what is this thing, this life, that makes the difference between a man and his corpse? Nobody knows. Nobody has ever known.

In the presence of the dead, man feels an overwhelming sense of his smallness, of his futility. It has always been so. The dead man has ever filled his survivors with a profound sense of helplessness. This man was. Now he is not. Yet the body is here. But the body is not HE.

One could have cut away his body—his legs, his arms, his nose, his ears, and yet HE would have remained.

The HE was here. It is gone. Where? It must be somewhere. But where? That thought filled primitive man with dread. This was something that he could not understand. And what he could not understand he feared.

Yes, the HE remained—somewhere. Probably nearby, too, because what purpose would it have in going somewhere else? Doubtless it would remain near the haunts that it had frequented in the past—near its home and its possessions. In that stage of human culture man had not arrived at the idea of religion as we understand it. He reasoned as our children might reason. And he was afraid—afraid of this HE that he could not see nor protect himself against.

Yet the HE could see him, of course. That made matters worse. What chance did a man have against a HE which could see him and which he could not see? Against a HE which could do things to him, perhaps, and to which he could do nothing? Clearly, the only refuge lay in concealment and flight.

So the survivors moved out of the cave where they had lived with the dead man; when he returned he would not find them there. Naturally, he would go looking for them; they would have to make themselves invisible. And here we come upon the beginning of our present custom.

138

Why We Mourn in Black

The Negroes of Africa, as a rule, have skins of a deep black. If they remained black the searching HE would find them easily. They must not remain black. Then what color should they be to evade detection? White, of course. So the survivors began to paint themselves with clays and pale earths. As Europeans mingled with them more and more, and taught these Africans the ways of civilization, the Negroes adopted some habits thus imported; among them was the wearing of clothes. Now, it obviously would be useless to paint the body white if this protective coloring were concealed by garments draped above it. They did the natural thing—during a period of mourning they donned white clothing. And to this day the Negroes of Africa's west coast wear white after a death.

The dark Aruntas of Australia, far less advanced in the scale than these Negroes, still go about almost totally unclad. And their mourning habit is to paint their bodies with white pipe-clay until the last ceremonies are finished—after which, as they believe, the ghost of the dead will have been laid, and the danger averted.

Painting the body white would do very well for a black man, but how about a white man? To paint himself white would make him even more conspicuous. No, the very opposite was required, of course. Our white ancestors, therefore, painted themselves black. In time they began to clothe themselves. They, too, saw the

139

absurdity of hiding the protective paint beneath a covering of clothes. Hence, reasoning as did the Africans, they rationally chose black as the color of their mourning dress.

To us, with our trained faculties, much of this seems childish. It is. We must remember, however, that in those far-off days all mankind was ignorant, superstitious, childish to a surprising degree as compared with ourselves. Admit that the first man had a brain as keen as ours, if we will, yet we must acknowledge also that he had not enjoyed the opportunity of training it. Our sixteen-year-old sons understand the radio better than we do; and poor grandfather cannot seem to grasp its working at all. So, little by little, mankind has learned; one generation—in a measure—picking up where the other left off. Thousands of years ago, then, our ancestors were ignorant; and ignorance is the parent of superstition.

Too, we must acknowledge the power of an accepted custom, even among ourselves. In our conventions, black is the proper attire among mourners. Without asking why, we have accepted the custom, merely because it was custom. If now, to illustrate the thought, we assume that at a funeral we were to see the women survivors of the deceased dressed in sky blue, and pink, and yellow, and the men in light gray suits and even knickerbockers, many of us would experience a sense of shock. Gossip would have it that these people were

lacking in a proper respect for the dead. Yet those
who so expressed themselves would find it difficult to
explain why they thought so; surely one can grieve
quite as heartbrokenly, one can respect with equal
feeling, in white or in black or in color. Suppose the
widow were poor and had but one dress—a green one.
Would she grieve the less sincerely for that? Even the
gossips would not maintain such to be the case. The
criticism would spring, we may be sure, not from the
enforced violation of the custom but from the volun-
tary violation of it.

If, then, among ourselves, public opinion is so strong
and the power of custom so potent that we continue to
observe the use of black, is it not easy to understand
why our forefathers, especially in remote ages, would
feel bound to follow the established rites? Yes, the
transition from black-painted bodies to black-dyed
robes was not a difficult step. Any other, indeed, would
have presented almost insurmountable barriers.

And, finally, burial customs persist for centuries
without change. Slow as mankind is to adopt radical
departures from habitual methods, even slower is the
alteration of a ritual. The funeral service of the Jews
includes a prayer known as the Kaddish; it extends
back into antiquity so far that its origin is not accurately known. The candles used at a Christian funeral
represent a custom inherited from the first followers of
Jesus, who were converted Jews; the early Jews bor-

rowed it from the Egyptians, probably through Moses, who was reared in the palace of Pharaoh; whence the Egyptians received it is not known, though their religious history can be traced with remarkable minuteness for more than five thousand years.

So persistent are funeral rites that it is safe to venture the statement that, if a nation were compelled to give up its traditional observances one by one, the last to go would be the ritual of the dead. It is not known when our ancestors first began to paint their bodies black to avoid the eyes of the peering ghost; nor would any of us care to predict when our descendants will eliminate the sable garb of mourning. For untold ages our fathers employed it, and so shall our sons for untold ages to come.

WHY WE ADMIRE AUTHORS

CAPTAIN MacBAIN and I were sitting in his office, talking to one of Mac's out-of-town customers, a Washington lady. In the course of telling us about her business the visitor remarked a little proudly, "You know, the wife of David Lawrence, the writer, comes to my shop regularly. She's one of my best customers."

Then Mac, who has a M.A. degree from two colleges and is an exceptionally bright and well-read man, turned to me and asked, "Do you know him?" I answered, "Heard of him. He writes for a big news syndicate and he contributes to the *Saturday Evening Post* and other magazines."

Bang! Mac's respect went up like the mercury in a thermometer that has fallen into the hot water kettle. There sat the lady, all puffed up with the idea that the wife of a well-known author was her customer, and Mac's chest sticking out farther and farther as he rolled over in his mind the agreeable thought, "This famous man's wife buys my goods—and likes 'em. Well, well, well! Isn't that great!!" I could almost hear him think it.

143

Why We Do It

Now, why? Why do people manifest such a high regard for successful authors? I don't know Mr. Lawrence, so we'll leave him out of the discussion. But I do know a number of other writers; and what there is about them to—but let's not generalize. We'll take a few specific examples. "Deac" Coleman is a good one to start with.

If you read the high-brow magazines you have doubtless seen a number of most abstruse and sage articles on psychology, signed by Loyd Ring Coleman. That's "Deac," which is short for "Deacon," a nickname applied to Mr. Coleman on the same principle that actuates us when we call a licorice-colored Negro boy "Snowball." If "Deac" is a deacon, then I'm the main muezzin in a Mohammedan mosque.

But if you had read any of "Deac's" articles and then were introduced to him you'd probably gaze in subdued awe at his cinnamon-tinted hair, his grave bespectacled eyes, his profoundly introspective expression. You'd listen to his drawly voice uttering his thoughts with the precise exactness of word-choice that such a man owes to his public. And then when it became your turn to speak you would, if you are like ninety-nine out of a hundred of us, try to say something intellectual—which would bore "Deac" stiff. He'd much prefer that you'd tell him that one about the clothing salesman and the girl at the cigar counter.

"Deac" has recently published his new book, "Psy-

chology—a Simplification," written in collaboration
with Dr. Saxe Commins. In it they use such phrases as
"unification of stimuli," "motivation value," "the in-
ertia factor as an element in calculable response."
Ugh! Naturally, when you first meet Dr. Commins
you would be tempted to say, "Doctor, the etiological
protoplasmic foramina of most pyrotechnic vicissi-
tudes are the apotheosis of trinitrotoluolic spondulix,
especially in northeastern Brazil. Don't you think so?"
But the distinguished author would a whole lot rather
hear you say, "Doc, have a stick of gum?"

I publish a little myself in some of the magazines,
and every now and then when I'm introduced the other
fellow says, "Oh, you're the man who wrote ——!"
And I can see that he thinks I'm almost as good as a
Congressman or a painless dentist, hence a person to
be regarded with veneration. But if he knew what my
wife could tell him—if he knew—if he knew!

So, taking them by and large, authors are pretty
likely to be just about as intelligent as ordinary folks,
and just about as irrational, and just about as cranky.
Yes, you could say for them without too much flattery
that mentally they're pretty average. And as for
editors—ooey!

Then whence this vast public regard for the man
whose name appears below a printed title as the
author?

Isn't this partly a display of self-love? All of us

can talk; writing is but putting talk on paper; therefore all of us could write for publication if we tried—
and magazine editors can testify that apparently most
of us try. Somebody has said that everybody has one
book in him, and all of us have deeply buried within
us the determination to write a great play some day.
Most of us, however, busy with other things and not
stopping to realize that writing is a manufacturing
problem—like producing $5 millinery for the Southern
trade or putting up a popular tooth paste—never get
very far with it, and regard the chap who does arrive
as close kin to ourselves. He is a mental giant of the
same intellectual stature as we are—only he's had a
little more luck.

Another factor that may enter into it is the almost
reverent faith that we give to whatever we see in print.
If it's in the book it's so. It follows, then, as the day
the night, that whoever wrote this unimpeachable script
shares in its exalted estimation. And, of course, besides,
whatever is notorious claims our eager attention. We
flock to see whatever is widely spoken about, whether it
be a movie star or a trained seal, a murderer or a
writer.

Summing it up, we are fairly well agreed, I suppose,
that authors are just like other people, no better and
not a great deal worse. There really isn't any moving
reason why we should rate them above other people, is
there? Of course not. And from now on we shan't——

Why We Admire Authors

Excuse me. My secretary just announces that the visitor outside is Homer Buckley, one of the great writers on advertising, and he's brought with him a famed fiction author whom he wants me to meet. Sorry I have to run away—but you know how it is.

WHY WE ARE PATRIOTS

FOR several months during the summer of 1914 my youngest brother had been traveling in Europe. Born in Texas seventeen years previously, the son of a naturalized German father, he was, like other true Americans, a devout believer that America is the greatest country in the world. The more he saw of foreign lands the firmer became his love and admiration for the United States.

Then the Great War let loose the mad wrath of hell upon civilization and this brother scrambled back to his country from Switzerland as soon as he could secure transportation. For several years after that his mind was dominated by the belief that Germany was the innocent and trusting victim of England's treachery. So deeply imbedded was this conviction that it remained unchanged until this country actively joined the Allies in 1917. Before our entry into the War Germany had been right; immediately thereafter Germany was wrong. Myself and another brother, both of whom had remained in the States during that year, had wasted many an hour of exhortation, argument and fraternal authority trying to convince the youngest that the

148

blame rested on the shoulders of the Teutons. He continued inexorably committed to Germany's snow-white freedom from culpability—until Germany became America's enemy and then, if he had been asked to paraphrase the Kaiser's pet combination, "Ich und Gott," I believe he would have worded it, "Der Kaiser und der Teufel."

Now, why? How came it that this American youngster resisted all the efforts of his brethren and family to convince him that Germany was in error, and then turned about completely when that nation became the antagonist of his own land?

His ancestry had nothing to do with it. The only mention of the old country that was ever made in our home was on the rare occasions—only two or three that I remember in twenty-five years—when my father recalled some apposite incident of his boyhood. But our father had died years before 1917; and our mother was of American-born forebears, with no interest in any foreign nation.

No, so far as I can make out, the truth was this. My brother, being of about high school age, had naturally mingled with foreigners of similar years; and, residing in Switzerland, a large proportion of those whom he encountered at his hotel were German boys— fiery, ardent and voluble. As all the world now knows, Germany was during that period industriously spreading skillfully doctored propaganda. Not only did the

Swiss press carry much of this, but German tourists hotly and loudly asseverated the Teuton's impeccability. My brother—young, impressionable—became so steeped in this brew of Anglophobia that he absorbed it into his tissues. Nothing could drive it out—nothing; until one day Germany became the foe of his own country, and then it simply vanished.

Since then I have become the possessor of a German history used as a text-book in the schools of Prussia. On reading it I learn that never has Germany been the aggressor in any war. Always and invariably she has been the gentle pacificator and the last to join in a conflict; never has she struck a blow until battle was forced upon her by enemies from the outside. With equal consistency she has never lost a fight; whenever a misguided nation has dared to trample on the rights of the sacred Fatherland swift and bitter was the retribution exacted by a just and jealous Deity. Gott had erected a "Verboten" sign on the borders of his chosen land and woe to the blasphemous and fatuous peoples who disregarded that sacred edict!

Is this feeling confined to Germany? Not exactly. Before me at the moment lies a copy of "La Patria Mexicana," by Prof. Gregorio Torres Quintero, of the Normal School of Mexico. This is the elementary national history taught to Mexican children. Its popularity is indicated by the fact that this edition (1912) is the eighth to come off the presses; doubtless subse-

quent editions have appeared since then for the instruction of the youth of our Southern neighbors. In it I
read of the perfidy of Spain which compelled Mexico
to revolt and win its independence by force of arms;
and there is something curiously reminiscent of the
German book in these pages. One chapter-head, for
example, reads in translation, "The Lawyer Rayon.
His Glorious Retreat to Saltillo." Not licked, you
understand; not routed in ignominious defeat. No—a
"glorious retreat." I wish I had a school history of
Spain's here to make comparisons!

There follow pages after pages of internal conflicts
—and always the side that ultimately triumphed seems
to have been in the right and truly represented Mexico.
Then the war with Texas, precipitated by Yankee
treachery. Texas was lost, but how? I read, "notwithstanding the surprise attack, the Mexicans made a
brilliant defence; Houston (the Texan leader), gravely
wounded in one foot and disconcerted by the vigorous
resistance encountered, ordered a retreat. But at that
moment one Mexican official fell dead, another dropped
wounded; one battalion fled, the left became disorgan-
ized, the confusion infected the center. Then the Texans
charged and by nightfall the rout of the Mexican
forces was consummated. . . . This disaster was of
no importance. . . . It so happened that Santa Anna
(the Mexican president, who led the army in person)
fell prisoner to the Texans the following day. . . .

Still, this success was but one of the incidents of the war. . . . But Santa Anna . . . thought only of himself. He issued orders to General Filisola (an uncaptured subordinate) not to attack the Texans and to retire; and this general, forgetting that never should the orders of a captured chief be obeyed, followed those of Santa Anna. This order, which meant the loss of the campaign, was worth his life to the prisoner. But this was not all. Santa Anna, without authority, recognized the independence of Texas. This earned him his liberty. Therefore that man was a bad Mexican, a bad patriot, a bad general and a bad president of the Republic." (Author's note—Nevertheless, Santa Anna was later entrusted with the Mexican army again.)

Then came the "Pastry War" through the licentious greed of France, succeeded by the "American Invasion," of which I read, "To the previous iniquities the Yankees added another; they claimed that the limits of Texas extended to the Rio Grande. Mexico maintained that the border-line was the Nueces River, farther north. And when some Mexican troops crossed the Rio Grande the Yankees exclaimed, 'Ye have invaded our territory.' And they pretended to be offended, placing the blame for the war on the Mexicans. Such were the charges which the wolf brought against the lamb in a well known fable."

And so on. Now, remember that the Mexican school children, taught this as gospel truth, believe it as long

152

Why We Are Patriots

as they live. As a boy in Texas I learned from my teachers the same story—but a little differently. Our version of it was that the cruelty of the Mexicans and their rapacity, comparable to that of England in her dealings with the thirteen original Colonies, finally forced us amiable Texans to revolt. And we Texans whipped them good and plenty. Against overwhelming odds our brave Sam Houston and his band of immortal heroes routed the multitudinous and better armed Mexicans into ignominious flight, captured their president and leader, Santa Anna, and compelled tyrannical Mexico to acknowledge our justly won and well-deserved independence. Hurray!

All of which means what? Nothing more than that we still carry into the present day the tribal habits of millenia ago without which civilization could never have become what it is. Back in the dim and misty antiquity of mankind our ancestors roamed the earth in small bands. If the members of such a migratory group felt no powerful instinct to fight in proof of their superiority over other men, that group was either soon absorbed into a more warlike tribe or wiped out of existence. Tribes could continue to exist as entities only if their members were ready at all times to battle off attacks. And men fight not with their friends but with their enemies. Thus it came to be that each tribe looked on other tribes as foemen. Friends were to be found only within one's own band. The friend who

153

Why We Do It

aided us was right; the antagonist who sought to slay us was wrong.

By conquest and absorption tribes grew into clans and these into kingdoms and these into nations. From countless generations of ancestors our modern races inherit their patriotism, their implicit conviction that their tribe, their nation, is and always has been in the right, and that they are the foremost people of the earth.

Gradually, with the growth of education and understanding, this will in great measure pass away. Then will dawn the time of true peace on earth. The men of those days will enjoy a warless world. Until that happy condition comes about men will continue in the unfaltering belief that their tribe is and always has been the best, that their nation is and of right ought to be the foremost power of the earth.

Meanwhile it is just a little bit comforting to reflect that, among all the dominant great white nations of the world, America alone remains the Undefeated.

WHY WE HAVE MONEY

FLAT-NOSE the arrow-maker was worried. He had made seventeen good arrows and needed but five for himself. What was he to do with the remaining dozen? That was one problem. The four little Flat-Noses were crying for something to eat; not that Flat-Nose particularly cared about them as long as his own tummy was comfortably full, but his wife always made herself such a vociferous nuisance when the children were hungry and there was no food in the reed-and-mud hut which the Flat-Noses called home. That was another problem. Two problems in one day; gosh, life was becoming complex!

Resignedly Flat-Nose stretched his arms upwards and backwards as far as they would go, yawned widely, and grunted. He was gathering up courage to go out and trade—a process ever abhorrent to the creative soul. Maybe there wasn't any hurry about it; this afternoon might do as well. Just then the youngest Flat-Nose let out an unusually piercing wail, Mrs. Flat-Nose's footsteps were heard approaching with a business-like patter and Flat-Nose made up his mind before his spouse could make it up for him. He grabbed

155

up his dozen arrows and marched out into the glare of the sunshine.

He strolled over to meet Big-Arm, whom he could see returning triumphantly from a hunt with the body of a deer slung easily over his shoulders. Big-Arm saw Flat-Nose and waved his hand in greeting, grinning broadly the while with pride. Flat-Nose concluded that useless effort was an economic waste and sat down on a rock to await Big-Arm's approach. "What'll you take for the deer?" he inquired, when the hunter came near.

"What'll you give?"

"Twelve arrows," offered Flat-Nose.

Big-Arm hooted. "Twelve arrows for a deer? The hide's worth that."

"Well, what'll you take for a hind-quarter?"

The two men dickered for a while and an exchange was effected. When the venison was on the fire at Flat-Nose's home, the children clustered sniffing and expectant around it, Mrs. Flat-Nose inquired, "How many arrows did you give for this meat?"

"Oh, we fixed it up all right," evaded Flat-Nose.

"Well, how many?" she persisted.

"Eleven, if you've got to know."

"Eleven? Eleven arrows for a hind-quarter? Elev— is it any wonder I have to pinch, and scrape, and struggle to make ends meet in this family? If that isn't an artist all over! We'll never get ahead in this world. Eleven arrows! You could have got it for six.

Why We Have Money

Don't you remember only the other day, when Red-Hair had fish, for three arrows I got——"

Flat-Nose closed his eyes wearily. The usual thing was on; it would last until the meat was cooked and eaten. And even then, he knew, he'd hear about this transaction for another round of days until the moon had changed twice or thrice. Women were all right—some of them—if they'd only appreciate the value of silence. Now, that little fat daughter of the widow Left-Hand, just growing into shy, retiring womanhood; she might be a likely, likable wife for a——Flat-Nose dozed off.

Ten thousand years have passed. We are at the present, but still bartering, trading without money. Your husband is, we shall say, a hardware merchant. How is he going to price his goods? How many ounces of butter shall he demand from a farmer in return for two door-butts, a hammer haft and an anvil? While he is puzzling over that an automobile dealer drops in and suggests, "I have a Buick demonstrator; how many gallons of paint and cylinder oil and kerosene will you give me for it, so proportioned that for every gallon of paint I am to receive seven and a third gallons of cylinder oil and thirteen pounds of kerosene —and I don't want any water in the kerosene, like last time, either."

Long, long ago men discovered that business couldn't be carried on in any such fashion as that. So gradually,

157

in one way and another, each tribe working out the method in its own way, certain standards came to be accepted as measures of value; everything else was priced in terms of that one standard. Thus, the first measure among many savage tribes having been skins, arrows may have been priced by their makers at one skin per dozen; a bow, first quality, well shaped and balanced, two skins; a grown daughter, especially good-looking and young and sweet of temper, 54 skins; another daughter, getting along in years, only fair as to looks, and peppery as to temper, half a skin; and so on.

As men ceased to be hunters and became cattle-raisers the whole animal was used as the measure, instead of only its hide. Things came to be priced at so many sheep, or so many head of cattle. In ancient Rome, to cite an instance, one ox passed as the equivalent of ten sheep. We can almost hear the Roman schoolboy sing-songing his tables before an impatient teacher, "Ten geese make one sheep; ten sheep make one ox; ten oxen make one—ten oxen—ugh!—ten oxen——" (Whack!)

It is remarkable how universally animals were used as money. The Icelandic law bears witness that cattle were so employed; various fines in the different Teutonic codes are quoted as payable with such-and-such a number of head; and on the other side of the world, in southern Africa, the groom buys his bride from her

158

Why We Have Money

father for an agreed quantity of beasts. One of our financial terms, *pecuniary*, is derived from the Latin word for money—*pecunia;* and *pecunia* came from *pecus,* cattle.

A truly wonderful array of objects has served as the medium of exchange in various lands. Slaveholding nations used their serfs as a measure of value; thus in old-time Irish law the price known as a *cumhal* is believed to have meant a female slave. In central Africa and in New Guinea captured girls are utilized today as trade-ins.

Other items formerly used as money were corn, olive oil, cocoanuts and tea. Our own American Colonists paid their debts with tobacco. The Indian wampum consisted of certain kinds of shells strung on sticks or animal tendons. The Fiji Islanders used whales' teeth, and among some South Sea tribes red feathers served the same purpose. In Abyssinia, as in early Mexico, a recognized medium of exchange was salt; the Aztecs, in addition, employed the beans of the cacao-plant, from which we secure our chocolate.

In time, however, the metals drove all competitors out of the field. Metals possess a number of advantages. For one, they offer small bulk in proportion to value— a feather quill filled with gold-dust requires less room than an ox and is easier to carry around or conceal. Again, metals deteriorate slowly, if at all, and thus allow themselves to be saved; a man can lay aside a chunk of silver for a year, or two, or ten, and it will still remain a chunk of silver; but corn or cacao-beans would fall prey to weevils, or rot, or sprout. Further, metals require no cost or trouble for their maintenance; a slug of copper, safely hidden away, entails no expense whatsoever to the owner; but its value in sheep requires daily food and care.

Almost all the common metals have been adopted as money at one time or another. Iron passed as currency in Sparta; even yet iron spikes serve as money in central Africa. In conjunction with copper, iron was so used in early China, and at one time the Japanese "small change" was coined of iron. In Burma they used lead. Under Montezuma the ancient inhabitants of Mexico used T-shaped bits of tin. We ourselves use copper, nickel, silver and gold.

Almost any metal would fill the requirements of a nation as long as its inhabitants traded among themselves. But when a lead-money Burman, for example, chose to trade with a silver-money Chinaman, how could each party to the deal translate his standard of value into the other fellow's terms? This typewriter which I am using at the moment, let us assume, cost me eighty coins of lead; you wish to buy it but you have only brass money—an alloy of zinc and copper. How many brass coins will you offer me? And how am I to know whether I shall be receiving my demanded price?

Why We Have Money

Clearly there had to be some one international standard, and gold has been chosen by most nations for the purpose. Gold does not rust nor otherwise lose in value through time or the elements; it is relatively scarce; when pure it is of one unchanging quality; it possesses small bulk in relation to its value; it is fairly evenly distributed over the earth. In many ways it fills the requirements better than any other metal, though some important peoples—like the Chinese and the East Indians—still prefer silver.

So everything, among ourselves at least, has come to be quoted in terms of gold. Your grocer will accept three copper pennies for a cake of yeast, it is true, but he does this only because for a hundred copper pennies the government will give him one silver dollar, and for five silver dollars it will give him a gold-piece. Thus the inferior metals, regardless of their intrinsic value, have a rating in proportion to gold and are exchangeable for it; they really are gold, so far as money-users are concerned; and because they are cheaper they present one advantage denied to gold— they can be minted in conveniently sized pieces. A penny's worth of gold, for example, is so small that it would be lost—and who could count out fifteen cents for an ice-cream soda if the golden pennies were the size of the quarter of a pin-head?

One curious result has followed this adoption of gold as the standard—of all things gold alone remains un-

161

changing in price. Wheat is worth fifteen cents a bushel more today than it was last month; iron is worth one dollar a ton less; beef-cattle are worth three dollars a hundred pounds more; but gold is worth precisely what it was last year and what it will be next year—almost exactly $20 an ounce.

That fact led to a scandalous swindle to which a friend of mine was an unwitting party. He owned, from 1906 to 1919, a low-grade gold mine in the West. When the War sent prices scooting sky-high all wages went up, of course, and at the current rates for materials and labor it was impossible to work the property gainfully. He had to pay more for what he bought, you see, but he could receive for his output only the same old price—$20 an ounce. Previously the gold, when refined and mintable, had cost him around $17 an ounce; but at the new price-level the cost of production had risen to $24 or $25, and naturally he shut down.

In 1919 he was approached by a stranger who offered to buy the mine. My friend was glad to get rid of it and, after pointing out the reason why he wasn't working it himself, permitted the buyer to have it at an agreed price. Whereupon the new owner issued a prospectus telling quite truthfully the enormous profits that the mine had yielded in the past, and sold shares "to enable the new stockholders to reopen the workings and once more start production." The prospectus was backed up by affidavits from an imposing list of mining engineers; in addition, the promoter had craftily secured from my friend a sworn statement of the previous profits, which he then used in his advertising. He sold hundreds of thousands of dollars' worth of stock, telling nothing but the truth and omitting only one important fact—that at today's production costs there is no possible way to make a profit.

So several thousand people now own stock in a gold mine which contains great quantities of gold—but they can't get it out except at a loss. The promoter has cleaned up a fortune and can probably never be punished, for he was careful to misrepresent nothing. And my friend, an honorable man, is being blamed by hundreds of cheated people whom he has never met because he lent his name—as they believe—to a robbery which has left many of them penniless, stripped of their life's savings.

WHY WE BELIEVE WHAT WE READ

YOU remember the old-time medicine-men—those long-haired, big-hatted dramatic chaps who used to gather a crowd around themselves on street corners at night and extol the merits of their nostrum for the edification of a gullible public. This particular operator, known as the Silver King, used to drive up to the public square in an old-fashioned covered prairie wagon, in the bottom of which—plainly exposed to view—were sacks and sacks marked with huge dollar signs and bulging with metal. Opening one he would dip his hand into it carelessly and cast out into the open space a glittering spray of coins—nickels, dimes and quarters. Then would begin his professional patter, while every now and again, with the most nonchalant manner conceivable, he would reach into the open sack and scatter into the air another stream of small change. In almost no time, of course, he had an eager crowd clustered thick within the sound of his voice, and then would begin his real business of the evening. Removing his broad-brimmed hat and sweeping back his flowing hair with a magnificent gesture, he would begin his magic formula. "Gen-tul-may-an," he would chant, "money is not the only thing in life. Helping suffering humanity to overcome its ills is greater than money. I have hee-yar a remedy which is a secret of the Kickapoo Indians who captured me when a boy. Did you ever hear of a sick Kickapoo? No-o-o-o—you nev-ver did—nev-ver! (Inasmuch as few of his hearers had even heard of the Kickapoos at all and knew as little about the Kickapoos as they did about the aborigines of New Zealand, the Silver King was on safe ground.) The Kickapoos are nev-ver sick, or ill, or ailing, or diseased. Why? Why are the Kickapoos nev-ver sick? I am asking you, gen-tul-may-an, why are the Kickapoos nev-ver sick, or ill, or ailing, or diseased? I will tell you. This marvelous medicine, made from Nature's roots and herbs, pre-vay-ants stomach trouble, liver trouble, kidney trouble, indigestion, rheumatism, gall-stones, pain in the joints, blood poison, lung trouble, consumption, cancer, catarrh, weak back, headache, intestinal disorders and tapeworms. That is why you nev-ver hear of a sick Kickapoo. That is why you nev-ver heard of a white man taking this marvelous remedy and suffering from stomach trouble, liver trouble, kidney trouble, indigestion, rheumatism, gall-stones, pain in the joints, blood poison, lung trouble, consumption, cancer, catarrh, weak back, headache, intestinal disorders or tapeworm. This marvelous remedy will cure those diseases for you, or I will give you your money back—ev-very

165

cent of your money—back. I guarantee that this marvelous remedy will cure your case, no matter how bad it is or how long you have suffered. That is the truth, gen-tul-may-an—the trew-uth. But don't bull-ieve me. Don't bull-ieve me. Don't bull-ieve me. Here is better proof than any man's word, gen-tul-may-an—better proof than any man's word. Here—look here—right here—where I am pointing. Here it is, gen-tul-may-an, printed right on the label. Read it for yourselves. Don't bull-ieve me. Read for yourselves. Here—right here— actually printed in plain black and white on the label. Do you want any more proof than THAT? Only one dollar per bottle, gen-tul-may-an, only one dollar per bottle. Step right up, my friends; step right up. Think of it, printed right on the la—ah, the gentleman in the blue shirt takes a bottle. Who's next? Printed right on——"

Now, whence comes this convincing power of the printed word? Why do we hoot a fellow-man to scorn when he offers us an incredible statement, and then open our mouths in astonished belief when he triumphantly produces a newspaper or book and points with victorious finality at the same allegation made in print?

I had a curious proof of this human trait only recently. Through a misprint in a magazine article I was made to say that I knew of a process by which gold could be extracted from sea water in paying quantities. For the next three weeks my mail was flooded with requests from readers asking to know more about the method. Occasionally such letters still straggle in. Every one of those inquiries breathed the most implicit faith in the truth of that mistaken assertion. In all, I received more than eight hundred responses. Then I experimented. I told my personal friends that I had found a way to mine the oceans for gold profitably. Invariably the claim was received with ribald incredulity. Whereupon I calmly extracted the magazine from my overcoat pocket, called attention to my name as author, found the right place, indicated the paragraph and handed it over to be read. It was delightful to watch the faces of those doubters turn slowly from cynicism to surprise and then to faith. With profound respect they would raise their eyes from the page and— with the most serious expression in the world—they would breathe reverently, "My gosh! Let me in on that."

My word, you see, when spoken, carried no weight against their better judgment. But the moment that I showed my same word in print they believed. Believed to the extent of wanting to part with their money. And, gen-tul-may-an, that is real belief, bull-ieve me.

For some time I have had a notion that this unquestioning confidence in the printed word is a hang-over from our school-days. During childhood there is so much to learn in this great world about us that we are

167

utterly credulous. As Bain puts it in his "Emotions and Will" (third edition, page 511), "The leading fact in belief is our primitive credulity. We begin by believing everything; whatever is is true." Our instructors teach, teach, teach; at home our parents verify these teachings. We believe. Among the things taught to us is the reading of print; and in all except the very primary grades that which we are taught is in print—our arithmetic, our geography, our history, our physics, our chemistry, our geometry, all are in print. Unconsciously we associate during those years the two ideas of print and truth. And, it seems, we never outgrow this association of ideas. Throughout all our future existence we carry firmly imbedded within us the urge to accept as fact whatever is in print. First we learn that truth is printed, and then we somehow appear to conclude that what is printed is truth. It is much as if a man should reason, "Thieves go to church; therefore those who go to church are thieves." Phrased in this way the fallacy of the argument is obvious. Yet, while we smile in tolerant derision at the charge that churchgoers are necessarily dishonest, we apparently accept unconsciously the conclusion, similarly arrived at, that print is truth.

There is this, however, to be said in behalf of our ready belief—it is fostered during later life by the scrupulous care of those entrusted with purveying the product of the press. Books, excepting those which are frankly fiction, must be truthful or they will find themselves denounced by critics and readers to such an extent as to make their publication unprofitable; so thoroughly is this understood by both authors and publishers that writers on serious subjects quote copiously from existing literature in support of their statements and theories, as is known to every reader of volumes on history, science, finance, and the like. Magazines are equally cautious; I have known a publication to return to a respected and trusted contributor an article on the habits of wild animals with the explanation that "the manuscript is intensely interesting but we fear that it will arouse disbelief of your accuracy among our readers." And as for newspapers, notwithstanding the haste with which they must be published, their accuracy is surprisingly trustworthy; lawyers acknowledge that there is less divergence among printed accounts of an accident or a crime, often gathered by reporters after the event, than there is between the testimony of sworn and honest eye-witnesses untrained in the rigorous school of journalism. If all of us made as few misstatements as the newspapers the world would be more veracious than it is.

This editorial insistence on strict truth nourishes our earlier conviction that whatever is printed is believable. And in this chapter we have an illuminating example of how unquestioningly we absorb as fact a statement which we see in type. In a previous paragraph I mentioned one Bain and his "Emotions and Will." Is there such a writer as Bain? Did he publish a book called "Emotions and Will"? Is there on page 511 of the third edition the remark which I have attributed to him?

I don't know. I lifted that bit of information from the Encyclopædia Britannica. But I believed it. Didn't you?

WHY WE BLUSH

THERE are some curious facts about blushing which almost everybody recognizes when they are mentioned but which few people ordinarily observe consciously.

First of all, we blush under three states of mind: shame, shyness and modesty. The reddening of the face during anger is not truly a blush and has a totally different origin.

Blushing, then, occurs only when our attention is directed to ourselves, and when we are subjected to the possibly adverse opinion of other people. Even when we are alone a blush forms because we think of some situation which might cause others to lower their regard for us.

Yes, even the expectation of being placed in such a position is enough to cause a blush. Thus when a modest woman is led to believe that a questionable story is about to be related her face may be seen brightly flushed. And this is doubtless due to her rapid reasoning that if the conversation takes such a turn she will then be ashamed to be seen listening;

anticipating that she may perhaps have cause to blush she blushes in advance.

Blushing is usually believed to affect only the face, ears and neck, and in the main this is true. Many people, while blushing intensely, feel the entire surface of the body growing hot and tingling; and this shows that the entire skin must in some manner be affected.

Even the interior of the eye blushes, as Dr. Burgess discovered while examining two albinos. In the back of the eye, opposite the pupil, the optic nerve spreads out into a sort of net which lines the inside of the eyeball; in albinos this retina is naturally red. But when these two subjects blushed the retina invariably increased in redness.

Dr. J. Crichton Browne had occasion to visit a lady who was quite shy; he found her in bed, whereupon her face flushed hotly. An examination of her lungs being necessary, Dr. Browne undid the upper fastening of the patient's gown. As soon as her chest was exposed the blush, which until then had been confined to her face, ears and neck, immediately extended down over a considerable area of the revealed skin.

A partly-clad Chinaman, aged 24 years, became ashamed in the presence of a European; his blush extended over the face, arms and breast; and another Chinese, when criticized for not doing his work better, blushed all over the surface of his body. In two Malays the face, neck, arms and breast were seen blushing, and in another Malay the blush extended down to the waist. Many Negroes have the skin too dark for a blush to be visible, yet mulattoes are known to blush; and on a very dark Negress, who had a white scar on her face, the scar was seen to turn red under circumstances which would have caused a blush to appear on ourselves. Many more instances might be quoted among various races. It is quite likely that all mankind blushes, and for exactly similar reasons.

Perhaps through lack of self-possession young people blush far more strongly and frequently than the old. Men and women, too, blush more easily and deeply when among the opposite sex than among their own. Young lovers, in the presence of each other, blush sometimes for no apparent cause except the continued gaze of the beloved; but even the slightest indication of disapproval from one will cause a most painful and long-continued flushing on the other. And when the offended one is afterwards alone, and in perfect darkness, the recollection of the scene is enough to warm the face noticeably, so strong and persistent is the resulting blush.

Before I try to explain just why we blush, let me relate some remarkable effects of the concentration of the attention. Dr. Bramwell describes several instances of true blisters being raised on the bodies of hypnotized subjects when they were told that the cold lead-pencil touching their skin was a red-hot poker. Other

173

writers confirm this by reports of similar experiments of their own. I myself have seen a young lady hypnotized, and while in this state her arm was touched lightly with a silver fork removed from its usual place for the purpose; she was told that it was a glowing coal. Within a few moments the supposedly burned area became quite red; and when the subject was awakened, although she did not appear to remember what had happened, she scratched her arm repeatedly and complained of a "scorched" sensation. On another occasion I saw a different subject hypnotized and told that her heart would beat quite slowly; a physician present counted her pulse and within a few seconds it dropped to nearly half its usual rate. Again she was told that her heart would beat rapidly, and her pulse ran up so high that another physician could not count aloud fast enough to keep up with it.

Ordinarily, of course, we cannot at will control the rate at which the heart beats. And while none of us may have tried it we probably feel a justifiable confidence that merely touching the wrist with some cool object under usual circumstances will not raise a blister nor even redden the skin. Yet perfectly normal people, while hypnotized, have exhibited those seeming impossibilities. Students familiar with the matter explain this as a result of the concentration of the subject's attention.

Here, then, we have two sets of well-authenticated

174

Why We Blush

facts: reddening of the skin when attention is strongly directed to a certain part, and blushing when we are under the scrutiny (real or imaginary) of people who may be looking at us in disapproval.

The parts of the body upon which the attentive gaze of others is most concentrated are the face, neck and ears; and they, as we have seen, are the ones on which blushing most frequently occurs. Yet when other parts are exposed—as in the case of the hospital patient and the half-naked Malays and Chinamen—blushing can take place over the arms, chest, and trunk, when attention is directed to them by the eye of the critical beholder.

An interesting confirmation of this may be secured from people who blush easily. With no third party present, direct your eyes to the floor and say in a gentle tone, "You are blushing." This will be contradicted by the subject, and a quick glance of your eye will attest the truth of the denial. Afterwards, when the incident is no longer freshly in mind, say again in exactly the same tone, "You are blushing." This time, however, gaze the subject steadily in the face a little while before you make the statement, and in a surprising number of cases you will be rewarded with a rich deep flush. Your tone and words were the same on both trials; the difference lay in the direction of attention during the latter experiment to the subject's face.

For that matter, fixing one's gaze on any part of

175

the anatomy of another may cause a distinctly noticeable response. This has come to my attention through an unfortunate habit of which I have in vain tried to break myself; when in deep thought I stare persistently (but unseeingly) at any little simple pattern such as the knot of a shoe-lace or a decoration on a bit of lace. Time and again I have been awakened from such a brown study in the street-car or other public place by the restless moving of the foot or arm at which the other person thought I was peering intently.

Calling attention to a blush is embarrassing, as it only intensifies the reddening and the discomfort of the sufferer. Disregard of the feelings of others is always unkind, but we ought to be especially considerate of those who blush. In this forward, bold world one who evidences shyness, shame or modesty is rare enough to deserve public appreciation, especially as the blush is one testimony of emotion that cannot be faked. The only trouble is that when such people discover that we are trying to save them from blushing they forcefully and promptly—blush.

WHY WE TEACH DEAD LANGUAGES

A WRITER, discussing a medical subject which might shock some more or less touchy people, and perhaps not wishing the vulgar to have a certain passage made too clear to them, adds the following information in a footnote:

"Et ego protuli super his afforismis quedam dicta que circumspexi et ea meo nomine nominavi et similiter protuli aliquos aphorismos aliquorum modernorum quos denominavi eorum nomine."

And Tylor, in his "Primitive Culture," with even less reticence boldly inserts this statement in the body of his text, apparently never dreaming that anyone would find it too frank or intimate:

Τῇ δὲ πατὴρ Ζεὺs δῶκε καλὸν γέραs ἀντὶ γάμοιο,
Καί τε μέσῳ οἴκῳ κατ' ἄρ ἔζετο πῖαρ ἑλοῦσα.

We shall revert to these remarks towards the end of the chapter. Meanwhile it might be well for us to consider just why we demand of our boys and girls that they spend valuable hours studying Latin and Greek.

All of us, of course, are familiar with the usual argument: that the study of abstruse subjects, even though useless in themselves, "trains the mind." So in pursuance of this doctrine I made it a point during the past few weeks to ask every college-trained man or woman whom I met, "In exactly which way does the study of Latin and Greek train the mind?" The only answer which I have been able to dig up is, "It teaches you to think." Which is, of course, merely restating my question and giving it as an answer; for training the thinking apparatus (the mind) is nothing else than training us to think.

I couldn't resist the temptation to point this out; and I inquired whether that sort of logic was a fair sample of the kind of thinking which results from studying dead languages. This was in every case indignantly denied, as might have been expected. The next question was, "Just how has your study of Greek and Latin helped you to think?" And the invariable response was, "Well, I don't know; but it helps."

So I went to a High School principal. He said, "The study of Latin and Greek does train the mind, just as athletics develop the muscles. Besides, acquaintance with those languages aids in the understanding of English, our own tongue." Here was something tangible, for our psychologists maintain that perhaps the best quick measure of a man's intelligence is his vocabulary and memory. Wherefore I inquired, "Well, the word geography is derived from two Greek words meaning earth-writing. In which way does that information

178

aid one in estimating the mineral deposits of Africa or
in understanding the cause of earthquakes, or in appre-
ciating the value of the exports of the Straits Set-
tlements?" Sadly the professor shook his head and murmured with a pitying, superior smile, "It does, even
though you don't understand how." But I do understand one thing—that the three divisions of my question involve three separate branches of science, none
of which is geography; and that little detail slipped
right past him unnoticed. If he had done just a teeny
weeny bit of thinking he would have discovered the
trap; but possibly he was so absorbed in the value of
Greek and Latin as thinking-helps that he had no time
to think.

Yet I tried him again. "You said, a moment ago,
that those studies help the mind as bodily activity
stimulates the muscles. Well, now, if you wanted to
teach one of your students to become a great baseball pitcher would you set him to chopping wood, and
running races, and lifting weights, and boxing—or
would you get him out on the diamond and train him
how to pitch a baseball? I notice that John McGraw
and Connie Mack and Bucky Harris, when they want
to develop a pitcher, do it by making him pitch; is it
your idea that a better plan would be to have him dig
a trench?" The principal answered, "No; but those
managers are teaching the recruit something specific;
yet the parallel holds, for a good early training in

179

boxing and running and chopping down trees would bring those young men to the ball-field strong and sturdy, ready to be taught the art of pitching and equipped to practice it well."

More questions followed: If that's the case, why don't managers pick laborers instead of selecting their pitchers from those who have already shown a marked ability in pitching? If the idea is that a weak man can be made so strong through labor that he will then make a good subject for a pitching-course, and that a man with a mediocre mind can have it trained by Latin and Greek to become a profound thinker, what chance will those upbuilt products have against competitors who came into the world naturally equipped with strong bodies and strong minds? Isn't it an absolute truth that intelligence cannot be increased in the individual any more than you can change the color of his eyes? Whereupon the school-man inquired acidly, "Don't you believe in education?" and walked away. I wish he had remained long enough for me to point out that there is a vast difference between schooling and education, as there is between intelligence and knowledge.

The intelligence of each individual is born into him; it cannot be increased. Perhaps I was a bit unfair with the schoolmaster. Yet one cannot help remembering that Sir Isaac Newton, the greatest mathematical genius who ever lived, was considered a dunce by his teacher; and that Shakespeare, the world's greatest

180

writer, had little schooling; and that Beethoven, the world's greatest composer, was considered stupid and unpromising by those who tried to initiate him into musical studies. Such examples could be multiplied.

Aha! Did you catch that Latin?

Multiplied—from the Latin *multus*, meaning "much, many,"—plus the same root from which we get *ply*ing a trade, or ap*ply*ing a *ply* of wood. So to multiply means to make many; how does knowing the derivation of that word help us with mathematics? Mathematics from the Greek μάθημα , meaning "learning" or "science." Now that we've had a little Latin and Greek it will help us to think better.

The truth is, of course, that the first writers of our own civilization were the old Greeks and Romans. In the Middle Ages the only available great literature came from those sources; one had to be able to read Greek and Latin or there was little of great consequence to read. So when the universities were founded about the year 800 A. D. they were faced with the necessity of teaching Latin and Greek, very much as the Chinese and Japanese feel they must send their young people over here to our schools to learn because the literature of the present dominant civilization has not been translated into those tongues.

Previously there had been elementary schools but they taught little except the rudiments. As the nobility and scholars and monarchs manifested interest in the

181

universities the latter became the pattern on which schools were modeled, because every schoolmaster wished his enterprise to compare favorably with the highly regarded universities. As nearly as possible the schools copied after the great acknowledged centers of higher learning; and the poor kids had Latin, and Greek, and algebra, and geometry and other outrages inflicted upon them.

That has come down to us. It isn't wholly the fault of the teachers, we must admit frankly. To illustrate: Suppose a man were to open a new school, asking that our children be sent there, and offering as an inducemen that he would teach no dead languages, no higher mathematics, no literature—only reading, writing, arithmetic, some history and geography, and the choice of a trade like cigar-making or house-painting or brass-founding. He wouldn't do much business, would he?

The few youngsters who are going to become professional people might need a dead language; doctors and pharmacists, to choose one instance, probably would require Latin to write and read prescriptions. But they are so few, and the children who go to schools are so many! Most of the pupils are going to be bookkeepers, and salesmen, and motor-men, and factory workers, and clerks, and contractors; learning those activities in school would perhaps be a real help to the majority; and of what benefit is it to them to be able

182

Why We Teach Dead Languages

to parse *ego sum* or to know the relationship of
π to r^2?

So we live in a business country and are schooled in
non-business subjects for the most part, only because
our ancestors did the thing that way. And we shall
continue blandly on our course for many years, so
powerful is the force of habit.

Oh, yes, I promised to say some more about those
two opening quotations. You have forgotten most of
your Latin and Greek, of course, so that translating
them for yourself would be a difficult task now, if you
could accomplish it at all any more. Unless you seek
out a school-teacher you will probably never know just
what those paragraphs say. Well, they aren't worth
the trouble. One is an admission by Moses Maimonides
that he has added some remarks of his own to a treatise
by Galen, and the other is a couplet describing how
the Greek goddess Hestia sits in the house of Zeus
receiving fat. Neither one will help you to sell more
shoes or to float a better coat of enamel.

WHY CHILDREN OBEY

A H, but do they?" objects some harassed parent. Yes, to the extent that their conflicting instincts will permit.

The child, we must remember, is bubbling over with the desire to learn. This is a wise dispensation of Mother Nature, a preparation for the adulthood which is to come.

In its own short life the individual child could never accumulate for itself the knowledge necessary for a successful existence, so it is born with the craving to gather information from those who have it. Quite properly and naturally the child turns first to its parents for such help.

How implicitly the child believes! Every little boy feels confident that his daddy is the superior of every other man; he will affirm stoutly that his father could beat Babe Ruth at baseball, Jack Dempsey at fighting; and if Pop wanted to swim the English Channel he could do it with one hand tied behind him. That same child's mother can sing better than any other lady in church, can cook better meals, knows all that is to be known and is never, never, never wrong. The

Why Children Obey

child may not agree with all of Mumsie's decisions, but even then he believes Mumsie is undoubtedly right.

In the presence of such unlimited knowledge and power the child does just what you and I would do— tries its best to learn from superior intelligence. The child knows no higher ambition than to be just like its parents.

But children are marvelously quick to detect sham. And once a child has gone through the misery of discovering that its parent is fallible, its little blind faith begins to waver; the parent's judgment is questioned. And then another instinct comes into play.

You see, if our children were satisfied to be exact duplicates of ourselves the race would never progress. A colt, for example, learns from its mother the things that can be picked up by imitation; after it has learned those it is, mentally at least, a fully matured horse. Never does it occur to the colt to reflect, "Mother is wrong in some of the things she does. I am going to do those things differently—and better." No, the colt docilely absorbs what its mother has to impart and seeks to know no more. That is why we find the horse the stupid animal that he is, and he will remain so until the last horse is dead.

Our youngsters at first, before they have a definite reasoning power, obey without question. We order, "Stay there," "Bring me that," "Spit it out," "Go to bed," and we are obeyed eagerly in most cases. This

185

quick obedience is necessary for the child's welfare. Without the instinct for obedience the child would soon end its career fatally in any one of a hundred different ways. So accustomed are we to childish submission that when we see a two-year-old baby which pays no attention to commands which it should understand we are likely to conclude that it is weak mentally.

But after the age of faith comes the age of doubt. The parent has been discovered in error on occasion. With the self-confidence of youth the child says to itself, "Mumsie may be right—but I think she's wrong. I'm going to take a chance and try it my way." That's the difference between our child and a horse's child. Our little one, tot that he is, feels within himself that he is a Man; he is going to tackle this great world a bit on his own account, pitting his intelligence against all tradition. He bumps a lot of skin off of his nose during his entire life in making these explorations into the unknown, but that is the spirit which keeps humanity moving ahead.

So here we have two opposing instincts—obedience, to assure the progress of the individual, and initiative, to assure the progress of the race. In the beginning there is manifested only obedience; later, at about the fifteenth year, obedience is often rendered most grudgingly; initiative largely takes its place. That is the trouble-making age. With budding maturity the earlier submission to authority returns again to somewhat its former estate. Thenceforth the individual balances the two motives, and how he employs them in any given situation forms a large share of what we term character.

Curiously enough, both these antagonistic impulses, obedience and initiative, may have a common ancestry. Those who have studied the state of mankind before history began to be written have offered us the Old Man theory. Back in the Stone Age, for example, a man would steal a female to be his wife. From time to time he would meet other males; as likely as not there would be a fight. The conqueror would herd the victim's females and children into his own family. Over them all he would lord it in true man-fashion. What he said was law. The women, the children and the young men would obey—or be thrashed soundly. Only by being a solid unit could such a group continue to exist, for ferocious animals and dangerous men roamed freely. Those who obeyed enjoyed the protection afforded by the group and the Old Man's prowess; the rebellious who absconded and struck out for themselves stood a good chance to die, in which case they would leave no offspring to inherit their boldness. It was the obedient who survived and left children who "took after" their parents. Thus the submissive ultimately would be in the majority.

In time the young males would grow up. Little love affairs would begin to develop. If the Old Man discovered these he would smash the offender in his wrath.

But the Old Man would be growing older and weaker; the young males would be growing stronger. One day the Old Man would start something that he couldn't finish. A young male, or some roaming Old Man of greater strength, would crack his skull with a club. Then the winner would become the Old Man of the family until another day, well in the future, when his turn would come to sink under a well-aimed blow.

There would have to be obedience, you see, for the average individual to survive; and there would have to be stirring in the blood of the young men the ambition to become an Old Man on their own account (just as the young women would feel the urge to break away from their mothers and to annex a male for themselves) or the family as then constituted could not have continued to exist.

It is quite as difficult to prove that things went on in just this way as it is to prove that they did not; but there is evidence to support the Old Man theory strong enough to convince some highly intelligent students that it is substantially true.

If, therefore, our child exhibits a lively tendency to distrust the Old Man's judgment, and sets up a series of investigations on his own account, we must remember that he is probably behaving himself in accordance with the instincts which he inherits from thousands of ancestors. And to these, of course, we belong— though whence he could inherit some of his traits is

188

a mystery, unless they come from the other side of the family. Certainly when we were children we never did such things! But if we should consult our parents on the subject I wonder what they would testify.

WHY WE HAVE PAPER

SU-MATTO, Overseer of the Royal Clay Pits of ancient Babylon, was pacing his apartment in patrician rage. For the third time in one moon complaint had come from the Master of the Library Scribes that the clay cylinders were gritty. This last remonstrance had been accompanied by a sharp hint from King Hammurabi himself that unless the Overseer proved more capable of supplying the required quality a change of executives might be thought necessary.

As Su-Matto strode back and forth he presented a striking picture. Tall and straight was his body. His black hair and curly beard, glistening with aromatic oil, contrasted sharply with the white of his crisp linen tunic. His arms, as he clenched his fists in fury, showed big and muscular, hairy. An ivory and gold-trimmed stool of cedar coming in his way he kicked it savagely across the room, splintering one of its legs with the powerful impact. A trickle of blood flowed from his skinned instep over a gold-buckled camel-skin sandal, yet Su-Matto marched on, teeth bared in fury, not in pain. Even in their writhing his thick lips indicated a temper easily aroused, easily assuaged.

190

Why We Have Paper

The crimson draperies before a doorway parted. In blanched terror appeared a Nubian slave, arms spread far before him, head bowed to the level of the hips. "He has come," whispered the black.

"Ha! Send him in."

"Aye, lord."

The slave withdrew backwards. Again the curtains parted, admitting a short swarthy old man with mud-caked cuticle; his cheap woolen robe, reaching barely to his knees, bore streaks and splashes of earth-gray. He was barefooted.

The Overseer halted on the instant. Darkly his brows gathered into deeper furrows, his nostrils twitched, as he gazed on the obeisant figure before him. From his leather girdle he drew a dagger.

"Come here. . . . Closer. . . . Closer." The trembling visitor dropped on one knee before his master, imploring hands raised in voiceless appeal for pity. Su-Matto thrust his flashing blade flat-pressed against the other's upper lip. "Smell that," he rasped. "Smell it. Smell it." The workman closed his eyes and sniffed obediently, loudly. His lips were white.

Su-Matto suddenly raised the knife high. He threw it with all his force to the floor where it clattered sharply and slid—zipp!—banging across to the opposite wall. The kneeling man winced with a quick intake of breath.

"Ha! You shrink, do you?" jeered Su-Matto in high-pitched jerky tone. "You know that knife should have gone into your heart this time, don't you? . . . Well, do you or not?"

"Yes, lordly master," murmured the crouching figure.

"Yes, lordly master. . . . Yes, lordly master," mimicked the Overseer, resuming his march. "Always 'yes, lordly master,' to my face. But in the clay-washing sheds it is different. Oh, yes, that's different." He stood still, glaring across the room at the miserable workman. "Yes, in the clay-washing sheds it's, 'Oh, let a little grit remain. What do we care?' That's what happens there, isn't it?"

"Most lordly master——"

"Silence!"

Su-Matto stooped to lift the dagger. "Nicked the point," he muttered; "for a dog of a clay-foreman. Come here." The swarthy man rose and approached, with downcast eyes. "Raise your chin."

"Most noble——"

"Raise your chin."

Swaying, sick on his feet, the old man obeyed with fluttering eyelids. Su-Matto lay the edge of his knife against the bared wrinkled throat. "How does that feel? Nice and sharp? Hey? In the name of the god Bel-Marduk I ought to slit your gullet for you." He paused a moment irresolute. Then he returned the knife to his girdle. "Well, live," he decided. "But if

ever another grain of grit—one single little grain, mind
you—is discovered in——"

"Master, I swear——"

"You lie. You're old and useless. Why didn't you
drive those slaves of yours harder? What are slaves
for? No—you won't do any more. Go back and work
at the washing-tubs with the slaves. Send that nephew
of yours to me. I'll try him as foreman. You—well, well,
don't cry. It must be hard to be old. I—you—I—well,
you shall remain foreman, then. But your nephew shall
have charge of all the work; he shall be called your
assistant; but his alone shall be the responsibility.
Would you have him die?"

The grateful gray-beard fell to his knees, his eyes
streaming. No sound came from his quivering jaws.
Su-Matto smiled indulgently. "Yes, you shall live and
keep the title of your authority. But *him* I hold to task
for the clay. Unless it henceforth be smooth and grit-
free——" He touched the dagger's handle significantly.
"Now go."

Such were the troubles of the Overseer of the Royal
Clay Pits in Babylon. For never had there been a
King like Hammurabi. Of all the monarchs that the
world had known he was the most learned, the most
interested in preserving the knowledge of his time.

From far and near he gathered wise men to his
capital. They brought the lore and the literature of
their native lands. He caused to be collected the judg-

193

ments of the courts, codified and indexed. The prophe-
cies of his astrologers were carefully preserved, as were
the histories of his predecessors. All these things and
many more were written down.

And this was the manner of the writing. A soft clay
biscuit or cylinder was indented with the tip of a little
shaft like an unsharpened lead pencil; on one flat end
the wood was chipped away, leaving a narrow wedge
upstanding. This left marks like slender sunken spear-
heads. Grouped in various ways these marks indicated
sounds, much as do the letters of our alphabet. Then
the clay was baked; it became hard like pottery or
earthenware. And of all the libraries that we know,
King Hammurabi's was the first. So perfectly did the
baked clay retain the writing that to this day our
scientists read these newly-discovered records that were
filed away more than 5000 years ago.

That sort of arrangement would do very well for a
city-living population where civilization was at its
height. But there were few communities the size of
Babylon. Most of the towns were small; in them there
was not enough writing done to justify a whole great
group of folks in supplying the needed clay, the washing out of the grit, the baking. In many localities, of
course, clay would be wanting, only to be had if brought
from a long distance. And in these small towns most of
the people would be raising a few animals—cows and
sheep. At least, just as in our own small towns, the

hides of those animals would be easy to procure at little or no cost.

Also, there was a huge roving population not fixedly settled in any one place; this would be the big cattle-raising class who would move their flocks and herds from place to place as pasturage became scarce or eaten down. Among them, too, it would be much easier to secure a soft-tanned hide, free from hair, than it would be to find the clay, and wash it, and bake it. For them it would be easier to carry about a rolled bit of hide than a heavy collection of clay bricks. So there came into being the practice of writing upon white-tanned hides—parchment and vellum.

That was the method employed by the ancient Is-raelites who lived in Mesopotamia long after Hammu-rabi had died. David, later king of Israel, was a shepherd boy. you remember, when he administered his one-round knock-out to Goliath of the Philistines. Saul, king before David, was a tender of livestock for Kish, his father, before his selection as monarch. Naturally, these village people would find animal hides more con-venient as writing material than clay. So they used skins, especially for their very important documents— history, laws, and the like. And to this day in Jewish synagogues the Torah—the Bible written in Hebrew characters by hand in the old way—is still preserved on parchment, the processed real hide of animals.

A long book would of course occupy more than a

single skin. So the separate sheets were stitched together, or pasted, into one long ribbon or belt. Each end was wrapped around a cylinder of wood, much as our window-shades are fastened onto a roller; by rolling up one end while unrolling the other the reader could find any passage that he wanted.

In Egypt, however, different conditions prevailed. In the first place, the bull was one of the sacred animals; and, by association, all flocks and herds were more or less respected, so that their hides were not to be utilized for indiscriminate purposes; an even stronger reason was that the fertile land of Egypt is confined to a narrow strip along the Nile; the produce of these acres was not sufficient, after feeding the people, to support a great many sheep or cows. But the river banks were lined with rank growth of a cane-like weed—the papyrus. The stem of this weed had a peculiar property; when beaten up with a liberal quantity of water its fibers broke, separated and matted, as little shreds of wool yarn will do when tumbled among themselves for a while. The pulpy liquid mass was spread evenly, left to dry and trimmed; then it proved to be a flat sheet of paper.

In fact, our word paper is truly the Egyptian word *papyrus;* omitting the gender-suffix *-us* would leave it reading *papyr;* and between *papyr* and *paper* there is more difference in spelling than there is in sound. Even today the English write, "His Honour did me a favour

Why We Have Paper

by letting me ride in his waggon," while our form is "His Honor did me a favor by letting me ride in his wagon"; yet we maintain that both languages are one. Words are what count; not spelling. Another title for the papyrus plant was *byblos*, from which is derived the name of the Book which to millions is the most valuable ever printed—the Bible.

The old Romans and Greeks, for their less important communications, used flat sheets of wood, like tiny table-tops. These were even known as tables; and our children, carrying to school pads of paper in the same shape, call their paper blocks little tables—table-lets —tablets.

The Greeks coated one side of their wooden writing tables with black candle-smoke; over this they flowed a thin layer of white melted wax. Then, with an instrument for all the world like our manicurists' orangewood stick, they wrote on the wax. The wooden point of the *stylus* removed the wax in its path, permitting the black to show through.

From this candle-smoke black is descended our customary choice of ink that is black. The Egyptians, never having had the wax-layer habit, used many colors. But once black writing on a white ground had become the accepted practice the ink-makers during the days of the succeeding paper era sought to obtain a good rich black. And black remained the standard ink-color until quite recently when fountain pens were invented.

197

A fluid containing lampblack will not flow freely in a fountain pen, but a blue-black mixture of acids and dissolved iron will; and now we consider a blue-black ink quite satisfactory. If this book were printed in a rich dark blue on yellow paper you would find the innovation quite startling; yet the blue would be quite as legible as black, and psychologists aver that yellow paper is easy on the eyes. Blue and yellow simply isn't being done—largely because the early Greeks had no paper and used a white wax-coated slab.

In Mexico, when Cortez the Conqueror came over with his band of Spaniards, the natives were using paper made from the abundant local reeds. And, like the Egyptians, they wrote with red, or blue, or whatever other color seemed to them desirable. Their writing was by means of pictures, and often they colored these in various ways, so that a sheet of Aztec writing looks like an illuminated manuscript.

Without paper, at once cheap and light, our civilization could not be what it is. A large share of our advancement through the recent centuries has been the result of comparatively widespread education; and this implies many books at a low price. Only paper could have made these possible.

The paper on which this page is printed was made from a tree. The wood is shredded into tiny bits, boiled and stirred for hours until the wood fibers have separated and matted; then the mixture is spread thin, the

Why We Have Paper

water driven out, leaving a flat layer of crisscrossed fibers, as you can see for yourself under a low-powered microscope. During the boiling certain bleaching agents are added to produce a fine even white.

So clay is heavy; skins are costly; wax tables are cumbersome and temporary; only paper is cheap, light and serviceable for all the uses that we demand of our writing material. To realize why paper is so universal we have only to imagine a conversation between two people on our streets—one of them a visitor from a foreign land.

Inquires the visitor, "Who is that man driving the wagon with the load of bricks?"

And we reply, "Bricks, nothing. That's a Western Union boy delivering a batch of rush telegrams!"

WHY WE BLESS A SNEEZE

KA-AA-TSOOOOOOOOO! Ka-tsoooooo!!"
And our German friend, in his deep bass voice, booms politely, "Gesundheit! (Health)" The American at his side murmurs, "God bless you."

But a few moments ago we coughed. Neither of our companions paid the least attention, except to ignore our distress in gentlemanly fashion. And, just before that, the German unfortunately had to hiccough; nor did he receive a blessing for it. Yet the sneeze brought forth good wishes.

Is that habit of offering a benison when a person sneezes just a German usage which we have adopted? Let us travel around the world a bit to investigate.

Zipp! Here we are in Africa. These tall fine-looking natives are Zulus. They are hardly overdressed, are they? In fact, one glance tells us that they are pretty close to being typical barbarians. Let us offer one a bit of snuff to make him sneeze. Give it to that muscular big chap with the rhinoceros-hide shield. He takes a pinch curiously between his fingers, wondering what it can be. He eyes it closely. Now he is about to smell it—just a min—ah! There he goes. "Ka-tsooo!"

200

Why We Bless a Sneeze

He smiles, rather happily it seems. Wonder why. Look—he is murmuring something to himself. What is he saying? "I am now blessed (we hear him utter). The ancestral spirit is with me; it has come to me. Let me hasten and praise it, for it is that which causes me to sneeze." And listen! He is praising the names of his forefathers, asking for cattle, and wives, and blessings. What a strange idea!

We follow him to his hut where his wife lies ill. He asks a friend whom he finds there in attendance, "Has she sneezed?" Silently the friend shakes her head to indicate no. The Zulu's forehead furrows in deep concern. "Ah," he worries, "the disease is great." Then he turns to his wife for confirmation. "It is true that you have not sneezed?" Just then her nose wrinkles, she inhales deeply, and forth bursts a lusty sneeze. She smiles in delighted reassurance, thanking the ghosts of her dead, "Ye people of ours, I have gained that prosperity which I wanted. I shall be well. Continue to look on me with favor." And now her little child, which has been watching in silent attention, sneezes also. At once the father, the mother and the visitor salute it cheerfully with, "Grow!"

Let us follow this husband as he visits a native sorcerer to have magic made for his wife's quick recovery. We find the diviner seated cross-legged under a tree. The Zulu explains the object of his visit. Receiving a fee, the sorcerer consents. Look—he begins his incantations. And the first thing he does is to force a sneeze. "Good!" exclaims the client, "the spirits are present." And the cross-legged man, fully agreeing, greets the ghosts by saying, "Makosi! (Lords or Masters)"

Zipp! We are in another spot in Africa—among the Amakosa tribe. These have been converted to Christianity. See, one of them has tested our snuff. He is about to sneeze. "Kaa-tsooooooo!" Hear him, "Preserver, look upon me." He sneezes again. This time he whispers, "Creator of Heaven and Earth!"

So the Germans did not originate the custom, did they? Then did they perhaps borrow it from the Africans? That seems hardly possible. Further examination of tribal customs may help us solve the mystery.

The Negroes of Old Calabar, when a child sneezes, are likely to exclaim, "Far from you!" at the same time making an appropriate gesture as if to throw off some evil. In New Zealand, when a child sneezed, a charm was said to avert disaster. And if on starting an expedition in the Tongan Islands some one were to sneeze, everybody would feel his heart sink—a more certain presage of ill-fortune could hardly be conceived.

Across the ocean in the New World the same queer notion was deeply rooted. Hernando de Soto, as we all remember, led an expedition of Spaniards into Florida only a few years after Columbus had discovered America. One of the Indian chiefs, named Guachoya, came to pay de Soto a visit, bringing with him a stately retinue of his own nobles and dignitaries. The two leaders made a striking picture in the hall of the building which had been assigned to the strangers—the haughty Spaniard with his long, pointed mustache, his plumed hat and silken garments; the Indian clad only in a gay blanket, his smooth hairless face touched with tiny spots of red, yellow and blue pigment, on his head a coronet of eagles' feathers. The followers of each stood at a respectful distance.

As the two conversed, through the aid of an interpreter, suddenly the chief sneezed. Immediately his people, intermingled among the Spaniards along the sides of the apartment, deeply bowed their heads, opened their arms wide, closed them again, chanting deferentially, "The Sun guard thee and be with thee." Whereupon de Soto in surprise called to his fellow-Europeans, "By St. James! Did ye notice? They salute a sneeze as do we. Do you not see that all the world is one?"

Our old friends, the Greeks and Romans, also found occasion to exclaim upon the venting of a sneeze. Petronius Arbiter mentions the Roman custom of saying, "Salve! (Greetings)" to one who sneezed. Observant Pliny asks, "Cur sternutamentis salutamus?— Why do we salute you when you sneeze?" And the Greeks hugely enjoyed quoting a proverb based on the story of the chap who had such a long nose that he did not make the customary remark, "Ζεῦ σῶσον," when he sneezed because the noise was too far off for him to hear.

In India a Hindoo sneezes. A bystander urges, "Live!" and the sneezer courteously responds, "With you." But another Indian sect, the Thugs, like the Tongan Islanders, deemed a sneeze the forerunner of bad luck when setting out on a foray; so much so, indeed, that their belief often compelled them to permit captured travelers (intended for execution) to escape.

The ancient Jews on sneezing quoted, "Tobim chayim—Good life!" The Moslem's formula, akin to the Amakosa Negro's or the Zulu's, is "Praise to Allah!"

And, to close the list, a French book of etiquette, published in 1685, gravely advises its readers, "If his lordship chances to sneeze, you are not to bawl out, 'God bless you, sir,' but, pulling off your hat, bow to him handsomely, and make that obsecration to yourself."

Diverting for a moment, you and I were taught as children to put our open hands over the mouth when yawning. "This," we were told, "is good manners." But just why should that particular action be good manners? Most of us didn't learn to cover a sneeze until our scientists recently discovered that sneezing scatters colds and other ills. We don't cover a hiccough at all. Then why cover a yawn?

Why We Bless a Sneeze

Interesting as all the evidence is, we have no room for it here. Just as a hint, though—when the Hindu gapes he must snap his fingers and repeat the name of some god; the Moslem remarks, "I seek refuge with Allah from Satan the Accursed," and covers his open mouth; the Persians consider that yawning and sneezing follow when a man's body has been entered by a demon; and the Tyroleans cross themselves lest some evil come into the mouth.

These last give us the key to the secret which connects all the many queer racial habits which we have been considering. Throughout the world the belief has been widespread that when we open our mouths the demons will jump in and thus gain entrance to our bodies. Because the idea has sprung up independently among so many different peoples it has naturally been expressed in various ways. But everybody everywhere covers a yawn to keep out the Devil, and when we sneeze the open mouth invites his Satanic Majesty to come in, too. It is impossible to stifle the open-mouthed sneeze without injury or pain, so lowly-cultured tribes call on their fathers to protect them, while among the more refined and civilized the bystanders invoke the beneficent powers to guard and bless the sneezer.

And so, because it has been done in that way for uncounted centuries, you and I must—must—ka—kaaa-tsoooooooooo!

"God bless you! Gesundheit!"

WHY WE HAVE BEDS

THE sun was a diameter above the jagged line of
mountain crests to the west of our new-pitched
camp when Wesley, our colored cook, lit his supper-
fire. Before he had time to serve the evening meal of
crisp bacon and corn-pone the sky had turned grayish-
lavender, then purple. Suddenly, as if somebody had
touched the switch, darkness dropped down almost fast
enough for us to hear it hit the ground. The stars came
out. It was night in the Texas hills. There are no more
glorious nights.

While Wesley commandeered the only lantern to aid
him in washing the dishes Dave and I lay drowsily in
the grass on our backs gazing upwards. The air was
beautifully clear. Above us the firmament arched like
an inverted black custard powdered with diamonds.
Ages and ages away, deep in the soothing immensities
of distance, the larger stars writhed like little flame-
tongues, licking and flashing in the sable vastnesses
of space. Then, so softly that we scarcely heard him
begin, Wesley's rich baritone started crooning, "Swing
low, sweet chariot." Dave yawned and stretched. It was
time for sleep. Across the valley a coyote howled. I

206

spread my blanket on the ground under the camp-wagon, snuggled down into its folds, tired, . . . relaxed . . . drifted off.

But almost immediately the night wind blew cold. Waking sleepily I took a tighter roll in my blanket, hunching myself together for warmth. No use. The chill crept in bitterly. I heard Dave get up and go rummaging in the wagon-bed. Then there came the sound of a shovel biting into the waxy ground. And I remembered.

Ever and ever so many centuries ago our savage ancestors roamed the earth, homeless wanderers. A hide, stripped off some arrow-slain animal, served them as clothing by day, as blanket by night. They, too, had suffered miserably from cold during the hours of sleep, as I did now. So they hunted out little wallows and gullies in which to bed themselves down; and later—oh, years and years later—some genius had discovered that a shallow trench dug into the soil would keep him warm. I had gathered this from a long-forgotten book; where Dave came by his knowledge I did not know; but the idea was good. When he had finished his digging I took the shovel, holed out a trough maybe two feet wide and a foot deep, spread half my blanket across the bottom, lay on that, covered myself with the other half and fell asleep again, warm and comfortable until the chirruping birds and the sunbeams woke us to another day.

Why We Do It

How necessity bridges the gaps of time! A thousand generations ago some rude and shivering forefather of mine, digging with a broken stick and sweeping the loosened earth away with his hands, had hollowed out a hole in the earth that he might sleep warm. And here was I, a part of the highest civilization that this world has ever known, doing exactly the same thing for exactly the same reason. That ancestor of mine had sense; without trying it no one can conceive how snug and gratefully warm is the ground he treads underfoot, and which to him seems cold and inhospitable.

Of course after a time my ancestor learned that he would sleep easier if he lined his trench with grass and leaves; even better, especially in winter, was the idea of using two hides—one underneath, the other as a covering. That was a capital stunt. I can imagine him, the next day after that epochal invention, going about among the neighbors one by one, in an offhand, casual, uninterested sort of way and saying, in that flat bland tone which a person adopts when he wants to brag about himself without letting on, "Nice day we're having today. But it's getting on towards fall now, don't you think? Oh, well—what's the difference? That idea of mine keeps out the cold, doesn't it? . . . What! Didn't I explain that to you yet? Well, well, well—I thought I had, long ago. Why, it's the simplest thing in the world. All you do is—aw, go on, you're trying to kid me. Of course you know about that little trick. My, my, it's so simple, so easy! I thought everybody knew about— Oh, surely I must have told you how to do it, didn't I? Think a minute——" And he'd go on that way, teasing his audience with his half-finished sentences, working up their interest to the boiling point, getting them hungrier and hungrier to know the mystery all the time—and making himself more and more important and consequential, too, every minute, of course. Yes, I'm pretty sure that my ancestor would act just that way. Why, I had an uncle——

That fur-lined scoop in the ground would serve splendidly in the cooler climates. But down south, along in Egypt say, there wouldn't be any need of keeping the cold out, particularly. There would be other things that would creep in, making considerably more trouble than the cold—tropical insects, for instance, and spiders, and every now and then maybe a snake. And the ground would be sandy and scratchy. It wouldn't be long before somebody would think of weaving the Nile rushes together as a mattress to keep the sand away from his skin. That's just exactly what they did. Such a clever device solved the problem of the sand; the uninvited visitors still kept snuggling in whenever they felt like it. And the ground made a fellow so darned hot underneath!

Somehow or other—nobody knows any more just what brought it about—it became the custom to spread

209

that bulrush mattress over a frame. This novelty consisted of four palm-poles fastened together in a rectangle about six feet by three. Between these palm side-pieces a wickerwork of palm-fiber ropes was wrought, and over that they spread their bulrush mattresses. The new arrangement allowed a free circulation of air underneath as well as above—a needed blessing in Egypt. So delighted were those old-timers over the improvement that they could hardly lift their new beds from the floor high enough; they supported the frames with tall carved wooden legs, raising the beds so high that steps were required to get into them.

The Babylonians and Assyrians took kindly to the hint. With their great wealth such a luxury could be made a thing of beauty as well as a convenience. They expended huge sums on their beds, decorating them with ivory, and gold, and mother-of-pearl. The rich folks, of course, didn't work—labor was for slaves; instead they loafed around during much of the day on their beautiful new beds, which rapidly developed into the "divan," on which the king or his officials would sit while listening to prosy, wearisome statesmen and lawyers. How long ago that was! Yet until the Turkish monarchy was overthrown a few years ago the throne room of the Sultan continued to be known as his Divan. What did Solomon say about nothing new under the sun?

Several centuries later we still find the Greeks, and

Why We Have Beds

after them the Romans, utilizing their gorgeously arrayed beds at mealtimes. Instead of seating the guests on chairs the host provided a couch for each one, and everybody reclined in whatever position kept him most comfortable while eating; though—according to the wall-paintings which survive in Pompeii and other places—the mannerly way was to rest your weight on your left elbow, taking up your food with the right hand.

And the really high-toned families, as we might expect, instead of shunting the beds around every day from bedroom to dining hall and back again, had two sets of beds—those in the sleeping apartments for night use and day-beds for the dining room.

So in our living rooms today we have day-beds—which we call couches, davenports, or chaises-longues—for the convenience of our guests, though we should be scandalized if one of them stretched out on it full length. We have to thank that Egyptian of a thousand generations ago for inventing woven rush mats which we have gradually converted into mattresses. And don't forget—we have to thank the sand-fleas and the heat of Egypt for raising our beds off the ground for us.

Speaking of beds—it's nearly midnight. See you tomorrow.

WHY WE WRITE FROM THE LEFT

WHEN you started to read this chapter your eye unconsciously slipped over to the left side of the page. You are so accustomed to begin your reading of each line at its left-hand end that to follow any other method would be a real burden. Try, for instance, to pick out the separate letters in this line, beginning at the right. You linger over each one slowly; its very appearance takes on a novel aspect. Moving in one direction your eye sweeps skimmingly along the line; it halts and stumbles in going the other way.

Obviously, then, the natural way to read is from left to right.

Ah, but is it? Let us ask this venerable gentleman with the long beard and the skull-cap. He is a Hebrew rabbi, educated and courteous. What does he say? What? No—impossible. Yes, he insists that it is so. The ancient Jews wrote and read from right to left. And that was the natural way, he maintains. For are we not almost all right-handed? And does not the hand most naturally start writing on the side of the paper nearest to it? And as for reading—King Solomon's scribes would have had a wretched time trying to decipher text from left to right, as we do. Such an outlandish way to read! Backwards! They would have hooted at the idea.

Well, anyway, we have established one thing—there is a natural direction for writing and reading—the horizontal; either left to right or right to left. But always straight across the sheet.

Ho, is that so? The oldest written history that we have is part of the Chinese literature. How was that written—left to right or right to left? Neither—it started at the upper right hand corner and ran down the edge of the sheet. A Chinaman writes his love-letter as we do a column of figures—from the top down. After his sweetheart has read the first column on the right she goes to the next, starting at the top and reading down again.

At last we have hit upon the natural way of writing—start at some point and go either across or up and down; but each line starts right next to the beginning of its predecessor and runs the same way.

Sorry, but that's not so. Look at this photograph of an Egyptian carving on stone; the original sculpture shows many votive offerings, each labeled with its proper name; and to avoid any chance of confusing one title with its neighbor the artist has written one legend from right to left, the next one from left to right. Here is the reproduction of a door; the inscrip-

213

tion is divided into halves; on one side it reads from right to left, on the other side in just the reverse direction. That was a real system. You paid the scribe your money and you took your choice.

Apparently mankind has written in almost every manner except in a circle. To the majority of nations, however, it seemed more simple to let the right hand move toward its own shoulder rather than away from it. Thus most of us, when putting the addition-line at the bottom of a column of figures, ordinarily make the mark from left to right, though there is no reason why we should not do it the other way if we wish. And so, in writing, our ancestors also started at the left and wrote toward the right.

The scribes who wrote thus taught their own method to their apprentices. Our civilization happens to trace from groups among whom the scribes started a line at the left. Wherefore our children are drilled in the same procedure. If we had adopted a purely Hebrew culture we should most certainly now be reading from right to left. And if the Egyptian hieroglyphics had prevailed, then——

Our final sentence   .siht ekil daer thgim

WHY WE CHEW GUM

OLD One-Eye had shot an arrow through a deer, and now he was enjoying the feast. Quite an elaborate menu lay spread before him on the floor of his cave—a venison hind-quarter; two roots of a tuberous vine that he had encountered in the forest; a handful of walnuts, small and armor-clad in their thick shells. It was truly a banquet fit for a birthday dinner, though since One-Eye had no means of keeping time he lacked the faintest notion of how old he might be, nor did such an idea as a birthday anniversary cross his slow mind.

But he did understand the joy of food. Fire hadn't been tamed yet; to One-Eye and his kindred the red flame was an enemy to be feared and fled from, not a servant to yield warmth and cook meals. So this summer day he sat down before food that was raw.

First he sawed off with his flint knife a bit of the venison-haunch. Now, the deer is not essentially a fighter; it subsists on non-resisting vegetation and protects itself ordinarily by flight. Therefore the leg-muscles, especially those in the swelling quarters, were tough and fibrous. One-Eye knew this, of course; deer-meat had always been tough and fibrous; what else could one expect? But it was nourishing, and good. So he chewed at it with his great strong jaws until each mouthful was finally reduced to a softness that might be swallowed. The chewing took quite some time; but One-Eye had more of that than of anything else.

In between the hunks of meat he bit off pieces of the roots. These, too, were stringy and tough, like most food. So One-Eye munched and chewed, the balls of muscles at the corners of his jaw knotting and relaxing in long-continued rhythm. After an hour or so One-Eye had eaten enough; so he finished up by placing the hard small walnuts one by one between his molars and cracking them as we would a peanut. Filled at last to his limit One-Eye stretched out on the floor of his cave, grunted a couple of times in sheer physical satisfaction and fell asleep. There was nothing more to do that day.

For unknown numbers of generations One-Eye's ancestors had lived on just such coarse food. By now, the course of time had developed the jaw-muscles enormously. Old One-Eye could have bitten off a mouthful of your fingers without much more difficulty than you would experience with a sprig of celery. So powerful was his bite that he did not even realize that his meat and roots were particularly tough; they were a bit more resistant than berries, that he knew; but what of it? The bones were tougher than the meat, for that

216

matter, yet he could crack some of the smaller ones
with his teeth to extract the marrow; not only he could,
but he did. Certainly some things were harder than
others; but what were teeth for?

Then some genius discovered how to tame fire. That
was good. Now one could sit around the leaping blaze
on cold nights and be soothed with warmth. On the
inside of the circle, near to the cheering fire where it
was most comfortable, would sit the men, of course;
behind them clustered the women; and outside, where
they would least disturb their elders, the children might
find room for themselves.

That outer circle was the liveliest. There would be
romping, and play, and quarreling, and often a fight
or so going on. Bones half-picked by the men, together
with other food for which the masters had no space
left within themselves, the women might have; and the
mothers passed back to their offspring a share of their
own portion. One child, more voracious than the rest,
or less liberally supplied, would snatch bones from
smaller children; if the disparity in size were not too
great the plundered one would give battle for his property. Sometimes both the combatants would lose the
precious prize; sometimes it would be used as a missile
or a club.

During one such fight a bone, hurled by its holder,
missed the head at which it was aimed. It hurtled over
the assembled adults and fell into the fire. Whereupon

217

Why We Do It

One-Eye snarled wrathfully and the affray quieted
down into silence. One-Eye and the other men watched
the bone sizzle and smolder; then nostrils began to
twitch; a delicious new incense floated on the air. It
smelled like food. One-Eye reached out for a stick and
scraped the roasting rib from the fire. It burned his
fingers as he sought to pick it up, and the others
laughed. One-Eye sucked his scorched fingers—tasted
the warm meat-juice. Ooh! Here was something new in
flavors. His mouth watered for the hot bone.

His fingers itched to clutch it.

But it cooled soon, and One-Eye, lifting it gingerly,
sniffed appraisingly. It smelled delicious. He took a bit
of the singed meat between his teeth for a test. Oh, boy,
it was good! In spite of having gorged he eagerly
finished it off, his friends watching in astonished silence
that turned to avid questioning. Yes, One-Eye assured
them, it was excellent. He bestowed the nearly-cleaned
bone upon Scar-Face. This collaborator confirmed the
report. And so came cooking into the world.

Many experiments followed. Roots thrown upon the
fire assumed a different color and flavor, just as did
meat. Eggs exploded, or cracked the shell and ran
down into the ashes; not so nice. Nuts turned black on
the outside, the meat becoming soft and mushy and
unpalatable. Wild onions lost much of their plump-
ness. But the worst failure of all was when one cast
the leaves of cabbage upon the coals; those shrunk up

Why We Chew Gum

into nothing and yielded an odor that aroused laughter and taunting.

Yes, meats and vegetables were the best to eat after having been thrown into the fire. One quality they then exhibited, besides the change of color and flavor—they became soft. Not that this made any difference to One-Eye and his friends; they would have eaten the food even if it had grown harder. But it has made a tremendous difference to us.

For during scores of centuries our more direct ancestors have eaten cooked soft food; during such a long period, in fact, that our jaws are actually growing smaller since the days of hard food have passed. Many of us have overlapping teeth because there is no longer enough space in our diminishing jaw for all of them to fit in properly, as our dentists so well know. With decreased size of the bone came also shrinking of the muscles, through lack of use; our jaw muscles on the sides are mere remnants of the great bunches which One-Eye possessed. Yet so strong is the power of inheritance that we still retain unconsciously the desire to exercise those muscles more than is demanded by the soft foods which we eat.

Here in America the children—those fearless food-testers—tried eating the oozing sap of spruce trees. They discovered that it wouldn't "eat," but it did offer a not unpleasant taste and enough resistance to give the jaw muscles agreeable exercise. Their elders—after

219

scolding the youngsters for initiating such a senseless habit—adopted the practice for themselves. Within a remarkably short time the formerly abundant spruce trees became scarce, so rapidly grew the demand for the gum. Other ingredients were added, to eke out the vanishing supply, but without much success.

Then, in 1867, a shipment of the sap of the tropical chicle-tree was imported with a view to its employment in manufacturing rubber. The result was far from satisfactory. But one of the workmen, a spruce addict, finding himself without the material for his favorite habit, tried substituting a morsel of chicle-gum. It worked. A new industry had been germinated.

For the next fifty years gum-chewing remained a rather low-caste diversion. Patrician mothers taught their children that gum was to be eschewed and not chewed; so the poor kiddies listened in grave silence—and chewed on the sly. Then came Wrigley with his widespread advertising. And in January of 1920, a statistician has computed, Wrigley alone sold more gum in that month than the entire chewing-gum industry combined had distributed in an entire year a decade previously. Now even respectable folks are seen chewing gum; if not in public, then at least in the privacy of their homes, and with a zest not exceeded by that of the proletariat. Advertising is a great educator and a most democratic leveler of ranks.

I do not know Mr. Wrigley, but he is said to be a

hearty good fellow. So I take the liberty of suggesting that, when he deems the proper time has come to erect a monument in commemoration of his industry, he include in the design the figure of Old One-Eye squatted on the floor of his cave and holding to his teeth the haunch of a deer, uncooked and stringy and tough.

WHY WE "DRINK A TOAST"

G OOD liquor," explains an old chronicler, "much improveth being serv'd purl'd, or elsewise hotte, some toast added thereto strengthening the flavour and delicacie. Ye Kinge's Guarde indeed, robust men for the moste part travel'd oft beyond other realms, drinketh not wine except it be with soppes of toast in goodlie quantitie."

Of course if the Kinge's Guarde wouldn't drink without a few slices of toast immersed in the potion neither would any other roisterer of note. They really imagined that the fire-browned bread bettered the taste of the wine—and in the wine that they probably were served at times almost anything would have helped the taste, if some of the modern amateur-made product is any criterion!

And how they drank to the ladies! The extreme to which this was carried on occasion is vividly illustrated by certain bits of gossip that have come down to us. Listen to this, regarding the time of His Majesty, Charles II:

"It happened that on a publick day a celebrated beauty of those times was in the cross bath, and one of

222

the crowd of her admirers took a glass of the water in which the fair one stood, and drank her health to the company. There was in the place a gay fellow, half fuddled, who offered to jump in, and swore, though he liked not the liquor, he would have the toast. He was opposed in his resolution; yet this whim gave foundation to the present honour which is done to the lady we mention in our liquor, who has ever since been called a toast."

One knows not which to admire most—the gentleman's gallantry or the lady's genteel modesty.

Yet the custom of drinking to the ladies is far older than civilization in England. The old Roman sports drank as many glasses to their mistresses as there were letters in each one's name. Thus to Naevia her lover drank six cups; Justina's consumed seven. If I had lived in those days it would have been just my luck to be in love with a damsel named Constantina Valeriana Prognosis, and how I could have gone through with that job I don't know. Used a thimble, probably.

Anciently it was a religious rite to drink to the gods and the dead. At the yearly festival of the Passover the Jews celebrated the Seder, at which a glass of wine was set out in case the Angel of the Lord should come. From such an original idea arose the Greek custom of permitting the gods to share in their drink, by pouring them out a bit of the liquor—the libation. The Norsemen drank the "minni" of Thor, Odin and Freya, changing their "toast" after the advent of Christianity to include the Saints. Both Greeks and Norsemen at their feasts drank to the dead. Intimately associated with drinking to the departed must have been the drinking to the health of living men.

Thus the Goths pledged each other with the cry of "Hail," itself an exclamation of greeting—"good health to you," shortened into "hail." Our word "health" is the condition of being *hál* (hale), safe or sound; hence "hole," now written with an initial *w*— "whole"; and to "heal" is closely akin.

Good hailers as the Goths may have been, our pre-English ancestors outdid them; and to our ears, accustomed to the kingship between "be" and "was," it does not seem strange that the Anglo-Saxon should have pledged his friend, "Waes hael (be well)!" How thoroughly they "waes haeled" each other may be judged from the present form of the invocation—wassail.

Ever there has been more or less ceremony in drinking to others. That over-quoted diarist, Samuel Pepys, enters this for the 19th of June, 1663, "To the Rhenish wine house, where Mr. Moore showed us the French manner when a health is drunk, to bow to him that drunk to you, and then apply yourself to him, whose lady's health is drunk, and then to the person you drink to, which I never knew before; but it seems it is now the fashion." In return, a Frenchman visiting England speaks of "the custom of drinking but half

Why We "Drink a Toast"

your cup, which is then filled up again and presented to him or her whose health you drank." And so late as 1856 Lord Cockburn records that "every glass during dinner had to be dedicated to someone. It was thought sottish and rude to take wine without this, as if forsooth there was no one present worth drinking with. I was present about 1803 when the late Duke of Baccleuch took a glass of sherry by himself at the table of Charles Hope, then lord advocate, and this was noted afterwards as a piece of direct contempt."

In the era that someone has described as B. V. D. (Before the Volstead Days) it was not uncommon for those drinking a toast to do so standing. It was commonly thought that this rising indicated a certain degree of respect, but its origin was far more definite than that, and more practical. Originally there were no separate glasses at banquets; everybody drank out of one huge cup or bowl which was passed around in turn, whence arose the expression, a "round" of drinks. Some of those old drinking-cups had a cover; and when a reveler drank he handed the cover to the man on his right, who held it in his dagger hand; the drinker and the cover-holder both rose, the imbiber being thus assured that his little diversion would suffer no fatal interruption. In England today it is a common custom at feasts for both the left- and the right-hand neighbors of the drinker from a loving cup to rise, a relic of the time when protection was necessary while a man had his eyes shielded by the huge chalice. Those were the good old days! You invited a man to "Waes hael," and then he found it a wise precaution to load up your knife-hand or maintain a body-guard while he complied with your friendly suggestion, to make sure that he'd keep the "hael" that he had.

None of us remembers it, of course, but time was when after a few rounds of drinks somebody in the company would feel inclined to talk. His example would be contagious, and pretty soon the entire gathering was mingling a medley of discussion that made it impossible to understand anyone. A "table-master" was therefore chosen, his duties being to allot to each one present a period theoretically free from interruption. None of us remembers it, of course, but under such circumstances a certain topic would come up for discussion quite regularly—the ladies; and one by one the guests would propose drinking the health of their nominees. Along about 1650, after that gay fellow, half fuddled, had imposed upon women the name of "toasts," the table-master took charge of that ceremony, too, and so became the toast-master.

Thus "buns" and "toast" became associated, even though today the lover who feasts upon the beauty of his dear lady drinks to her only with his eyes.

WHY WE HAVE TOBACCO

A ND Moses spake unto all the congregation of the
children of Israel, saying, This is the thing
which the Lord commanded, saying, Take ye from
among you an offering unto the Lord; whosoever is
of a willing heart, let him bring it, an offering of the
Lord . . . oil for the light, and spices for anointing
oil, and the sweet incense. . . . And every wise hearted
among you shall come, and make all that the Lord hath
commanded . . . the incense altar, and the anointing
oil and the sweet incense. . . ."—Exodus, 34.

All in all, the Old Testament mentions sixteen aro-
matics used as incense offerings. The old Egyptians
had many more. The carvings of ancient Nineveh por-
tray priests with pots of incense. It was in use among
the Greeks and Romans, as well as in the rituals of
other nations. So we find it no occasion for surprise
that the Aztecs of Mexico utilized the fumes of an
aromatic herb in their temple ceremonies. In fact,
among most of the American Indians this herb was
considered sacred, and its smoke was held to be an
acceptable sacrifice, ascending into the air to the abode
of gods and spirits.

Why We Do It

But what did astonish the early explorers of the New World was to see the natives burning the herb in crude bowls which they held in the mouth by means of a pierced stem. This apparatus in their language was named a "tobaco." By the confusion of terms which is so common among visitors to a strange land the herb itself became known among the Europeans as tobacco. And such it remains now to all the world.

All of us remember the interesting story of how Sir Walter Raleigh was the first to introduce smoking into England; and how his servant, seeing his beloved master smoking for the first time, immediately assumed that Sir Walter was burning up; and to prevent the calamity threw a bucket of water over him. That is a dramatic and picturesque story; the only trouble with it, as in the case of so many striking incidents that we carry with us as fact, is that it is not true.

The first to bring tobacco to Europe was Francesco Fernandez, a physician sent by King Philip II of Spain to investigate the products of the new world. This was in 1558 and a few years later Jean Nicot, the French Ambassador to Spain's neighbor, Portugal, sent some of the seeds to Catherine de Medici. It was only a generation later, in 1586, that smoking implements and materials were brought to England, and the bearers were Ralph Lane, first governor of Virginia, and Sir Francis Drake. Lane was the first English smoker. What Sir Walter Raleigh did was to intro-

Why We Have Tobacco

duce the use of the weed among a little clique of Elizabethan courtiers. I wish we knew the truth about the cloak and the mud-puddle.

Thus is credit misplaced in a careless world. Raleigh had nothing to do with introducing tobacco to England, yet as long as smoking continues people will probably go on repeating the servant-and-bucket tale. Lane, who really first brought it to Elizabeth's realm, is known to but few people; while Nicot, who never visited America and did but dispatch a few seeds between two European cities, is immortalized by having the plant's extract named after him—nicotine.

The plant was at that time believed to have marvelous healing properties. It was called "herba panacea," and "herba santa." But man has always been more ready to minister to his pleasures than to his needs; where one interested himself in using tobacco as a remedy a thousand found delight in the soothing relaxation that followed smoking. Within less than a hundred years indulgence in tobacco had spread to almost every civilized nation on the face of the globe. And that in spite of the most resolute efforts to suppress it.

Statesmen thundered invectives against its use. They described with unblushing frankness the physical effects which tobacco wrought upon our bodies. Not an insane child nor a cripple was born but that its calamity was attributed by them to a tobacco-using progenitor. Not a criminal was convicted but that his degeneracy was proclaimed a result of the use of the "filthy weed." Grave authorities lent the weight of their opinion to the statement that what had held the Indians in savagery was tobacco. Finally the movement became so strong that some of the Church Fathers became convinced; laymen passed laws against the sale, transportation or possession of tobacco; and certain priests, misled by demagogues to believe that the souls of their parishioners were endangered, did all in their power to oppose the fast-growing habit, until a thorough investigation proved that the peril had been fanatically exaggerated.

Of course the anti-tobacco laws have long since become a dead letter, as has the opposition to so many other human wants, like anthracite coal, and potatoes, and railroads, and bananas, and spectacles; few citizens of Boston, for example, know that less than a hundred years ago it was against the city law to bathe in a tub except by advice of a doctor! I know one elevator boy there who apparently believes that the law is still in force, or else his doctor does.

Excepting, perhaps, its development as an insecticide we moderns have found no new uses for tobacco. In 1555 the natives of Brazil were described by a European as rolling the dried tobacco leaves into a small cylinder enclosed in a leaf of corn or palm—obviously a cigarette. The present-day Mexicans still roll their cigarettes in corn-shuck. The cigar, of course, is but a thick cigarette wrapped in tobacco. A Franciscan who accompanied Columbus on his second voyage in 1494 recorded the taking of snuff by the Indians. Chewing was first seen by a European in South America in 1502. And pipe-smoking had been in existence even at that time for so long that it had become a recognized ritual among all the North American tribes during their councils and peace-meetings.

Every one of these forms of indulgence has been enjoyed by Europeans. In cigars, pipes and cigarettes tobacco is still in common use. Chewing has become less widespread than it used to be, or at least less noticeable, but is by no means extinct. Snuff-taking, once among the fashionable accomplishments of the highest courts of the Old World, was for a time so popular that sovereigns presented a jeweled snuff-box to those whom they chose especially to honor.

Tobacco, like coffee, is unquestionably employed for its effect upon the nervous system. There is something in the nature of man which makes him enjoy a change of his nervous states, which in their very make-up are unstable. Even the most profound grief and dejection in time cease to bear upon us so heavily; and any source of joy or happiness, if indulged too frequently or too prolonged, fails to yield its ordinary gratification. Human beings find pleasure in stimulating or soothing their nerves from time to time, as a relief from monotony. The simplest way to achieve such a change is by the use of mild natural products, among which must be numbered tea, cocoa, coffee and tobacco.

Physically, tobacco probably has done mankind little good and little harm; psychically, its devotees declare, it has been a boon and a blessing. That it meets a universal human want is clearly indicated by the remarkable rapidity with which it spread over the nations of the world immediately after it became known to them. Our own individual views of its use are largely a matter of habit, as a friend of mine in Honolulu once made clear.

He does not smoke, but his wife does.

His little daughter had been sent to the birthday party of her dearest playmate. Previously she had encountered very few strangers and this festivity was quite an event in her young life. After she had been brought back home she came running to her mother in consternation, exclaiming, "Oh, my goodness gracious! What do you think happened?"

"I don't know, Marjory. What was it?"

"Oh, my goodness gracious! Guess."

"Heavens, child, don't keep me in suspense. Tell me."

"Oh, my goodness gracious! Florence's papa smokes."

WHY WE LIKE DIAMONDS

HOW unbearably hot it was that afternoon on the South African veldt! Away in every direction stretched the yellowish bare plain, touched only here and there by a bit of dusty gray-green bush which threw its shadow like a splash of ink across the burning glare. Earth, bush and shadow quivered and wriggled in the dancing heat-shimmer. Hot, hot, hot! The sun poured its savage rays down out of a sky of pitiless pure blue, unflecked by even a wisp of cloud. High in the air wheeled a hawk, eagerly eyeing the parched ground for a glimpse of moving prey. But in vain. Nothing would venture forth into that furnace; nothing, that is, except man. The hawk overhead saw, inching painfully ahead of a cloud of billowing dust, only the wagon of a traveling peddler. Disgustedly it slid away to more promising fields.

The peddler, gasping in the heat, sat on the wagon's seat with elbows on knees, his blue shirt open at the neck. Every few seconds he lifted the torn straw hat, resting like lead upon his brow, to wipe away with a saturated bandanna the wet that ran into his eyes. His mule, plodding patiently along with drooping head,

233

showed broad split streaks of lather wherever the harness touched its hide. To add to the general misery the wagon creaked disconsolately.

So they had traveled since sun-up that morning, the man and the mule. Every passing minute seemed only to increase the baking heat. Not for ten hours had either tasted water; both throats were dust-caked and dry. To the man it seemed that he had been going on thus since eternity began, that he would go on thus forever. His forehead throbbed. To close his eyes was the only relief; yet he could not bear to keep them closed—somewhere hereabouts there was a farm and a river—water. He must keep a-watch.

Creak, creak, creak! The wagon swayed from side to side in the rutty road, interminably. Incessantly, like hammer blows on the head, the mule's hoofs dropped with a regular plomp, plomp, plomp. No earth, no sky, no world—just glowing heat everywhere and forever.

Then something happened. Up came the mule's head. It quickened its weary tramp, stepped into a tugging walk, began lumberingly to trot. The driver sat up straight and peered about him. Doubtless the animal had smelled water. But where?

Ah! Over there where the wisp of smoke showed. There would be the farmstead of the Van Niekerks. The peddler swabbed the trickling streams from the back of his neck, from his throat, from his brow;

flipped the right rein in encouragement to his mule, set his hat at a firmer angle. Was this a breath of air filtering across the veldt or did it just seem cooler because there was rest—and water—in prospect?

Van Niekerk welcomed the stranger as befitted one who brought news of the outside world, tales of recent happenings, horseshoe nails, buckles, the needs of one's every-day existence. "Here, Jan," called he to one of his children sitting round-eyed on the porch of the farm-house, "take the man's mule for water and feed." He turned to the tired visitor who slowly unfolded his aching joints, "And you come inside for a cup of tea and a rest before you eat. I'm glad to see you. Did you bring any harness-buckles? Is it true that Lincoln ended the war in America two years ago, in 1865? Hi, you look tired!"

That evening, refreshed and plump-bellied, the stranger sat with the family in the cool yard before the house. The sun was barely setting, yet a grateful breeze had sprung up. Frau Van Niekerk swung on a rocker sewing a shirt for little Jan. Her husband, round and pudgy, smoked a long-stemmed pipe. "So your name is John O'Reilly," he rumbled in a deep basso; "any kin to the O'Reillys in Queenstown? No? Well, I thought maybe. Hey, children, be careful. You'll hit somebody with those stones."

O'Reilly, his chair tilted back against a tree, watched the youngsters in amusement. The elder was trying with his sling to hit a hawk that hovered high above in the purpling sky. Once he threw, twice, in boyish impotency. O'Reilly, trying guest-like to make himself agreeable, called to the youngster, "Here, Jan, let me have a try. Perhaps I can get him for you."

Reluctantly the boy handed the visitor his sling and a smooth stone. The man, starting to fit the pebble into the leather, halted in surprise. He brought the stone closer to his eyes, examining it curiously, incredulously. "I—what—where did you get this?" he asked in astonishment.

"In the gully, with the rest of 'em," replied the boy, carelessly. "Why?"

"I—well—of course I'm not sure, but—in the gully?"

Old Van Niekerk interposed. "What's the matter with it?"

"This looks to me like it might be a diamond," ventured the peddler.

Van Niekerk laughed uproariously. "Diamonds! In the veldt?" he thundered. "Ho, ho, ho! That's good. Diamonds. Ho, ho, ho! In the veldt! Mamma, did you hear? In the veldt. Diamonds. Ho, ho!"

O'Reilly slid his fingers over the stone. It felt dry but soapy. As he held it up to the waning light he made himself believe that beneath the gray frosted surface he could catch gleams and flickers of light. "Well, of course I might be wrong," he admitted craft-

236

ily; "but I'm willing to take a chance. Tell you what
I'll do. You pick anything you want out of my wagon
up to five pounds sterling and give me the stone. What
say?"

Little Jan bawled, "No, it's mine,"

Papa Van Niekerk became alert for business. "Jan,
you hush up. I'll buy you a pocket-knife—maybe.
Mamma, you go pick you a nice dress. And I want
some harness buckles."

"Here's a penny, Jan," soothed O'Reilly to the
indignant boy. "Got any more stones like that?"

"Naw," snapped Jan. "That's all. I slung the rest
of 'em at the hawk."

Old Man Van Niekerk was right. Diamonds! Why,
the only place you could find diamonds was in India.
And then maybe one in a month or two, which a monarch snapped up. Who else but an emperor could own
a diamond? Oh, yes, he had heard talk of a few being
unearthed in Brazil, which was part of the United
States north of the state of Canada, but these were
mostly brown and black stones, full of flaws. Diamonds! In South Africa? "Hurry, Mamma, before he
changes his mind. It's a trade."

Some days after that Dr. Atherstone in Cape Colony
was saying to an elated peddler, "O'Reilly, you're a
lucky man. It's a real diamond. I can sell it for you if
you'll take six hundred pounds."

O'Reilly did a sum in mental arithmetic. "Three

237

thousand dollars," he whispered to himself. "My gosh! Three thousand dollars. All right, Doctor, sell it for me, will you?" He sat down, fanning himself with his hat.

Diamonds! Diamonds! Only kings and a few favorites of fortune could have them. Diamonds! Thousands of well-to-do-people had never even seen one of the glittering gems. And here they were now to be picked up out of the dirt. No wonder South Africa went wild. Without waiting for further confirmation men swarmed across the veldt to the farm of old man Van Niekerk. Trusting souls! To them a mere rumor was enough. They dropped all business in hand. Into the plains galloped wild-eyed horses, urged on by frenzied drivers in the wagons behind them. One man decamped without sending word to his sick wife and babies. Another, appealed to by his brother to be taken along, slashed his pleading twin across the face with a rawhide quirt and fled along. Diamonds! Diamonds!

And it was true, true. There, in the raw veldt, buried in yellow soil, lay the precious stones, waiting for the first hand that might turn them up to the light of day. At last men could be rich without working. They killed, and plundered, and pillaged. Diamonds! Diamonds! Never had the world seen so many. Diamonds!

Yes, never had the world seen so many. Even to this day that soil gives up its glorious jewels in quantities that seem destined never to end. And still there are not enough. For the diamond, with its superb flash and iridescence, is the king among gems, fit only for a queen.

Ah, there's the secret. For the number of queens is endless. To each loyal, adoring male heart there is but one queen in this world—the girl of his dreams. And she must, of course, have a diamond, his gift and pledge. Who cares what the old chemist said?

With his knife the chemist had carefully split a lead pencil lengthways, removing the slender black rod within it. This he laid on his work-table alongside a lump of sugar and a diamond. Gravely he turned to the visiting bride at his side and inquired, "Which of these three would you rather have?"

Gazing at him for a moment in puzzled wonder the bride laughed. "Don't be silly," she chided.

"But I mean it," insisted the chemist. "All three weigh exactly the same. If you had your choice which would you pick?"

The bride bridled. "The diamond, of course," she grinned hopefully.

"Why?" asked the chemist.

"Why? Why? My sakes alive, anybody would."

"But why?" persisted her host.

"Why? Huh! You couldn't wear a bit of sugar in a ring, could you?"

"Exactly," answered the chemist, "these three things —the sugar, the graphite from the pencil and the diamond—are all pure carbon. They are the very same element in different forms. And you have chosen the rarest and least useful. Carbon as sugar we can use as food. Carbon as graphite we can use to preserve our thoughts in writing. But of what use is a diamond?"

"What use?" gasped the bride in scandalized amazement. "What use? Pooh! It's easy to see you never were in love."

Yet the chemist was entirely in the right. Carbon crystallized as sugar or as graphite can be bought for a few pennies per pound, and these both serve man's ends usefully. The same carbon, crystallized as a blue-white shimmering diamond, costs thousands upon thousands of dollars per pound, and cannot profitably be employed at all, in industry, except to cut glass (which hardened steel will do) or bore holes through rocks in the earth, or polish another diamond.

And the bride also was entirely right. Can anyone imagine a fiancée's heart leaping in proud delight because her lover has slipped onto her finger a circlet of platinum clasping in its dainty prongs a black chunk of lead pencil?

It's a rather warming thought, isn't it, to close our eyes and vision a blushing and dry-throated young man in the jeweler's shop this afternoon, selecting the emblem of his troth which he intends to offer to the light of his existence tonight at half past eight? He

240

must have something, naturally, to express his sentiments, so why not a queen's gift—a diamond? Only a cynic would remind him that from a chemist's standpoint a carat of lump sugar would replace the solitaire. The young lover values the diamond because it is rare, because it is expensive, because it is beautiful—and because when he offers his chaste and fretting fiancée a solitaire set in chased and fretted platinum he endows her with something that all of us may not have; he makes her one of the chosen of the earth; he gives her the concrete evidence with which to back up her implications to us and to her friends that her young man is successful and a comer.

Not that it makes any difference to him what we think. He has before him only one person's opinion, only one pair of eyes, only one pair of lips. If he satisfies that one opinion, awakes a sparkle of happiness in those eyes, is rewarded by the loving pressure of those lip—come, come! Away! Two's company, three's a convention.

WHY WE NAME THE BABY

THE lecturer had been under way for nearly an hour. He was going strong. There seemed little likelihood of a rest before midnight. We who had been inveigled by our wives into attending were heartily sick of the whole performance. The professor's subject gave him splendid opportunity to enlighten and interest. But he only drawled along, sprinkling on his tired audience sleep-inducing statistics and derivations like drowsy drops of ether. "Name, from the old English *name*," the droning voice went on, "a term common to all the Indo-European languages. German, *Name;* Greek, *onoma;* Latin, *nomen;* Sanscrit, *naman;* Spanish, *nombre;* French, *nom.* All of which, as we understand, ladies and gentlemen, signify 'name.' " Whereupon some harassed soul in the back of the hall, burdened beyond endurance, shrilled across the intervening heads, "A name! A name! What's in a name? A nose by any other name would smell as sweet. What's the name for good-night?" Which was rude and discourteous to a really great scientist.

For our custom of naming children has a long and curious history, well worth knowing. So I shall try to tell you what the professor told us, only as he is a most erudite personage I shall have to give it to you in my own way, without mentioning paleontology, or gens-nomenclature, or intra-tribe totemism, or some of the other terms that he handled with such facility and familiarity.

We have already learned how the Jews and other Semitic races, whose social unit was the family, named sons after their fathers. Thus Abou ben Adhem was Abou, the son of Adhem. At the time of Christ the Jews were subjects of Rome; and the Roman social unit was the clan, or gens. That is why the Jews distinguished themselves as B'nai Yisroel and their conquerors as gens-men—the sons of Israel as against the gens-men, the gentiles.

Those who adopted the Savior's faith were baptized into their new religion as a token of spiritual rebirth. Since all the new-born were customarily given a name at the baptismal ceremony, these Christian converts took on fresh appellations as a symbolic act. One who had been called James now became Joseph, or Jesse, or David. This is the reason why we say that Dennis, for example, is Mr. Murphy's Christian name. We also state that Mr. Murphy, not being a Jew, is a gentile, which is not true; for nowadays nobody belongs to a gens, even though in the South a few of the older folks still use some such reference as, "That is O. Hugh Diddit; his father is one of the Owensboro Diddits and his mother was a Pomfret, of the Putnam County Pomfrets, related through the MacLarens to the Abernatheys of Charleston."

But of course naming is centuries and centuries older than the Christian era. Nobody knows exactly how the procedure did originate, but enough has been rescued from oblivion to justify us in reconstructing the first scene, perhaps not very much unlike the actual happenings. The bull-necked cave-man, returning from the river-bank, stormed into the lair where his wife was nursing the most recent baby. From the look on his face as he stooped to enter the low-hanging entrance-arch she knew that her lord was in no soft mood. "What's the matter?" she inquired gently.

"Matter! I'll matter him," snarled the irritated husband. "Where's that boy of yours?"

"Which one? The baby here?"

"Naw, not the baby. That one with the flat nose. He took my best shell fish-hook, durn him."

"Flat nose? Well, all of them have that, you know. Do you want the red-haired one?"

"If that ain't a woman all over! Ain't the whole gang of 'em red-haired? They take after your mother's folks. Your mother's brother was certainly the red-headedest—where's that kid? The one that always yells so loud."

"Yells so loud? Well, if you can tell which one of them makes the most racket you're good, you are. I declare, all day long I've had the splittingest headache, between the baby, and the smoke from that wet wood that you brought in last night, and those youngsters out there shrieking like——"

"Where's that boy?"

"*Which* boy?"

"You wait till I lay my hands on him! You'll know then which it is. The one we had first. The big one, with a lip like a rabbit's. There he is outside now. Hey—you—Rabbit-lip! Come here. Where's my shell fish-hook? What! You broke it? I thought so. (Pow!) That'll teach you to let people's fish-hooks alone after this. Anybody with a rabbit-lip——"

The other kids looked on in delight, from a safe distance. After that little domestic drama, of course, the boy was known to his mates and their elders as Rabbit-lip. The innovation proved to be a big convenience. Pretty soon everybody had a name. And as a baby was born the natural thing was to give it a name, too. In fact, among some present-day barbarian tribes, the baby is named even before its birth; the father and mother go proudly about, describing themselves as the parents of Dew-Drop, or East Wind, or Morning Star, or some other child which has not yet come into the world.

These birth-names were often chosen with some thought of connection with the name of the parent, as we name our race-horses; thus Mr. Whitney's

Whiskery is the son of Whisk-broom. A man named Bright Sun, to take an example, might call his first boy Dawn, the early morning light being obviously the offspring of the solar disc. If the mother's name were Summer Moon the daughter's might be Crescent.

Or Moonshine.

Other methods would have a place, of course. Among these was the plan of giving the youngsters numbers, as we do with convicts. The natives of the Adelaide district of Australia still adhere to this system. They attach names to their children in the order of age; the first being *Kertameru* (meaning One), the second *Warritya* (Two), the third *Kudnutya*, and so on. The Malays follow a somewhat similar arrangement, calling the first-born *Sulung* (Eldest), the next *Awang* (Friend or Companion) and ending with *Kechil* (Little One) or *Bongsu* (Youngest). In Madagascar we find the same tendency: *Lah-imatoa* (First Male), *Lah-ivo* (Intermediate Male), *Ra-fara-lahy* (Last Born Male). The Dakota Indians called the eldest son, through a comparable habit, *Chaske;* the second *Haparm;* the third *Ha-pe-dah;* and so down the list. Those who recall the companion-song to Hiawatha, so popular twenty years ago, will recognize the name *We-no-nah*—the Dakota Indian's way of numbering the first-born girl.

The original names, whether derived from those of the parents or whether in effect numerals, were changed

246

as frequently as might be prompted by the ripening age or exploits of the individual. Another active cause, especially among the number-using races, was the confusion that necessarily followed the division of such few names among so many youngsters. If, for example, a Malay mother should stand at the door of her hut with a fine ripe plum in her hand and call to her own son, enticingly, "Sulung! Oh, Su-u-u-u-lung!" every first-born boy within eye- and ear-shot would come chasing up in the ardent conviction that he was the Sulung who was meant.

As the boys of the primitive races emerged into adolescence they underwent ceremonies admitting them to full standing in the tribal councils, just as the Jewish boy of fourteen becomes ritually a man after passing through the Bar-Mitzvah or a Christian lad takes on a new status after Confirmation. The savage boy would have revealed to him at that time the secret lore of his people; he would permissibly assume the use of arms for warfare and would have a new name bestowed upon him. If his prowess became conspicuous he could pretty surely count on achieving a more distinguished title—Killer of Three, Blood Drinker or some equally charming designation. This persisted into almost recent times, as witness Charles the Hammer, King of France, who gained his first fame in battle; so King Ethelwulf of England was really "Noble Wolf"; and Jack the Giant-Killer, though a legendary character, illustrates with what readiness the untrained mind accepts a denomination from an exploit. The untrained mind, did I say? Do we ourselves not have our "Home Run" Kelleys, our "One Round" Hogans, our "Honest Daves," our "Bath-House Johns"?

Personal appearance, especially peculiarities or deformities, would have a strong influence. We have all read of Eric the Red, Long John, "Three Finger" Brown, "Lefty" Louis, "Fatty" Arbuckle. In my boyhood one of our Texas military heroes was "Big Foot" Wallace, though whether he was so christened in infancy the book did not state.

Nicknames of all sorts are freely bestowed and readily accepted. Among our boys the terms "Carrots," "Skinny," "Shorty," "Snooty," "Boney," "Lanky," "Cinnamon," "Curly," and dozens of others are conferred without malice or indignity. In fact, the acquiring of a generally acknowledged nickname bears with it a trace of popular distinction. There are lots of Henrys but only one "Beany"; plenty of Sams, but one "Greasy." Understandably the possessors of these honors appreciate their good fortune. They have ceased to be one of a swarm; uniqueness, individuality have descended upon them by the unanimous consent of their fellows. They stand apart. Primitive man felt the same way about it.

Another origin of nicknames was the danger of hav-

Why We Name the Baby

ing one's real name known to enemies. With that in their possession they could work magic against us as surely and as powerfully as if they had secured a finger-nail paring or a lock of our hair. For several weeks during one summer I and a friend were in the daily company of a Kickapoo Indian known to us as Poti. He received many kindnesses at my hands and came to regard me so highly that later he made a journey of some four hundred miles without my knowledge to do me a favor. Yet, though he admitted that Poti was "just a call," as he phrased it, he refused to divulge his real name to me then or ever. And when I discovered that "Ta-a-a-ah!" in his tongue meant the equivalent of "No," or "Stop," or "Quit it," and asked him to confirm the interpretation, he would not deny the truth in my question—but he would not admit it; there might be a chance for magic even in that. Who could tell?

Not only among barbarians but with ourselves it is quite common for a name to continue from father to son. A highly successful children's doctor has said that he gains the confidence of his little patients through calling them by name; and it is his observation that when he must guess he is fairly safe in addressing the youngsters as "Junior." Among the Palestinian Hebrews it was expected of a man that he marry his childless brother's widow, "that thy brother's name may not die out among Israel." The pre-

249

sumption is strong that the first man-child of the woman was to be called after her first husband.

They didn't worry about the daughters.

In the Alaskan district the Kolosh Indian mother sees in a dream the dead relative who has transmitted his soul to the little baby about to be born and whom the child will resemble; quite obviously the child inherits the name of the deceased as well as his appearance. If among the Old Calabars a child is born soon after the death of one of his brethren the newcomer is supposed by the mother to be her lost young one returned, the name thus being rebestowed as a matter of course. In Guinea when a child bears a strong resemblance to a dead kinsman the latter is presumed to have come back to earth in the new body, and his name is conferred upon the little one. Among the Khonds of Orissa the tribal priest appears before the child on the seventh day after birth, dropping rice-grains in a cup of water to divine which of the baby's ancestors has thus been restored to earth, that the recovered soul may be given its proper name. In New Zealand it was the custom for the priest to recite to the infant a long list of names so that the baby, by sneezing, might indicate its own selection. Somewhat similarly the Cheremiss of Russia would shake the newcomer until it cried, repeating names to it the while until by ceasing to wail at any particular utterance the child had named itself. Both these latter practices were doubtless an expedient by

250

which the reborn soul was permitted to establish its identity.

Sometimes a single baptismal name may be used for a whole group of separate individuals who have nothing in common except their nativity or occupation. Thus in the War whenever our soldiers spoke of the enemy he was known as "Heinie," a diminutive of *Heinrich* (Henry). To us all Chinamen are "John." And every Pullman porter is "George."

We have room for but one example of how an honored name may be perpetuated even though there be no blood tie. Christ was preceded by one widely respected John, the Baptist; and His "Beloved Disciple" was another John, the Evangelist. From this beginning it has come to be that among ourselves John is perhaps the commonest of male baptismal names; this is true of its forms in other languages—of Ivan in Russian; of Juan in Spanish; of Ian in Gælic; of Jean in French, of Johann in German; of Joannes in Latin; of Giovanni in Italian; of Jan in Polish; of Joao in Portuguese; of Ioannes in Greek; of Janos in Hungarian. The original form of the name is the Hebrew Yohanan, meaning "Jehovah has been gracious." Among female names its counterpart is some form of Mary—Maria, Marie, Maryan, Marian, Maritza (Little Mary), Marija, Miriam—in commemoration of the Virgin. Among Spanish-speaking races this latter tendency is so pronounced that one often is

251

introduced to a gentleman whose baptismal names, chosen in all reverence, are Joseph Maria.

Clearly, then, in the beginning children had to be named or numbered as a matter of convenience; also, the human delight in assigning a nickname quickly established the habit of fastening on the growing child some other title, chosen to fit its appearance so as to make identification easy—Long-Nose tells us a great deal more about its human possessor than does Robert or Benjamin. Personal descriptions in the Bible are few, but Esau's appearance so struck the chronicler's fancy that we know him to have been red and hairy; had he become a great national hero he would undoubtedly have descended to us as Esau the Red-Beard, as did Friedrich Barbarossa (*barba*, beard, from which we derive "barber"; *rossa*, red, ancestor of our "rose" and of the "Rosi-Crucians," Knights of the Red Cross).

In recent times, with the growth of population and the complexities of civilized life, registration is usually demanded at the time of birth or baptism. I have rarely met a person, though, who was satisfied with his or her given name. And, while the law permits people to change their names at will, in the absence of fraud, very few take new designations. So we do not start a boy out as Number Seven, alter him to Cry-All-Night, then to Big Joe and finally Enemy-Killer. No, we entitle him Thomas Alva Edison to start with and

252

that is expected to last him for all his days—but still we who admire his achievements affectionately dub him "The Wizard of Menlo Park." And Lincoln is "Honest Abe" and "The Emancipator."

How those old tribal customs do persist!

WHY WE USE A WEDDING RING

ALEXANDER, rising conqueror of the known world, lay soddenly on the royal couch of Darius in the palace at Ecbatana whence the Persian King had fled before him. He was drunk as Noah, having spent the whole night in wild debauchery. His usually white and ruddy complexion was now the pasty color of raw dough. His eyes, normally melting and hypnotic, were closed in heavy slumber. The leonine mane of hair which so captivated his admirers now drooped, wet with perspiration, over his high forehead. He breathed heavily, alarmingly like a man suffering a stroke of apoplexy.

Two Macedonians, trusted guards, stood fully armed at the door of his bedchamber. The sound of approaching footsteps aroused their attention. One of them, Philotas, stepped forward a pace to beckon with his spear for silence. Still the intruders came on, though more quietly. Four heavily armed infantrymen were conducting between them a Persian nobleman, elegant and effeminate-looking compared to the bronzed muscular rudeness of the Greek soldiers. One

254

of these spoke to the guard. "An envoy from King Darius to Alexander."

"Alexander sleeps."

The first speaker scratched his head in perplexity. "He says his message is of utmost importance, as near as I can make out. And he must see Alexander at once."

Quizzically the guard smiled upon his countryman. "Well, then, suppose you go in and wake him," he suggested.

The other tossed his head in dissent. "No, not for all the Persians in the world," he retorted; "I value my life too much. Well, his nibs will have to wait." Turning to the foreigner he spoke a few words in halting Persian. The dainty nobleman shrugged his shoulders in patrician submission to fate.

Just then Alexander stirred. At the sound the guard sprang silently to his place at the door. A muffled groan issuing from the bed, he gazed in at the form of his master. Alexander was struggling to a sitting position. "Water," he gasped, "water, fool. And hurry!" A white female slave, captured in a previous battle, had been awaiting the call. She sprang to the leader's side, pouring out a fresh cool stream of spring water. Alexander drank deep, demanded more, laved his face and head. Then he caught a glimpse of the stranger outside. "Who is that?" he demanded. He ordered the visitor before him.

"Who art thou? And what is thy errand? Curses on

255

this Persian heat! Water here! Well—answer. Who art thou?"

The Persian dropped to one knee. "An emissary from Darius, O King," he replied softly.

"And where is thy authority?"

The stranger, drawing a ring from his finger, handed it to Alexander. The youthful conqueror glanced at it carelessly, was about to return it when something caught his eye. He examined it more closely. "This is what?" he inquired harshly.

"Thou seest, O King; the royal seal-ring of Darius to serve as my credential. Is it not the custom among the Macedonians to entrust the monarch's seal-ring to an envoy in proof of his authority?"

Alexander laughed harshly. "Yes. Also it is the custom to execute any who forges such a token. This ring is newly engraved. Never has this ring been used as a seal. It is a forgery."

"Oh, King, I swear——"

"Swear to thy master, the lord of Hades, whom thou shalt meet right soon. Ha, welcome, Philotas. Thou comest in good time. Here is a forged ring for thee to play with; have me this liar beheaded at once. Hey—water! Where is that wretched slave? Water, I say!"

In those long-gone days only kings used seal-rings. The possession of these symbols by others was punishable by death. This strict law was necessary, for the monarchs were unable to write; their signature was appended to a decree or other document by means of the royal signet-ring, from which employment the jewel gained its name. Nor could other officials read; so an authorized ambassador carried his lord's ring as proof of his proxy. Imitation or forgery could be prevented or minimized only by the imposition of death. Ignorance begat murder.

Thereby the first signet rings became associated with the idea of a promise of true performance. Soon after the death of Alexander his kingdom split up in numerous separate divisions, each under the sovereignty of one of his many captains. These new rulers, too, assumed royal rings. Their courtiers followed the custom. It was not long before rings were a universal ornament, once the strict taboo had been broken down. The more lenient the monarch the further down into the ranks of his people extended the custom of wearing signet-rings. And thus any metal finger-band, once merely an ornament among the nobles, assumed the significance of a contractual obligation when given to another.

After the ring had begun to serve as a token of the promise to marry it is not difficult to understand how it would also come to be used as an evidence of the completed contract. And as soon as some married women began to wear a ring others would demand one also, as visible proof of the legality of their rela-

257

Why We Do It

tionship with the husband. In those days of slaveholding, we must remember, a wife would probably
welcome some conspicuous evidence of her position,
lest she be mistaken for a concubine.

At first the proud owner wore her wedding ring on
whichever finger might be dictated by her fancy. The
opportunity for sentiment, however, was too tempting
to be lost, so doting husbands couldn't resist the impulse to suggest that the ring be worn on the left hand
—the heart's side. And then a real poet improved the
notion in putting on the ring. He touched with it each
finger in rotation, saying at the first, "In the name of
the Father," at the second, "In the name of the Son,"
at the third, "In the name of the Holy Ghost," and at
the fourth, "Amen"; and there it remained from that
first June day through all the anniversaries that
followed.

Why did brides choose June? We have the Romans
again to thank for that. May was an unlucky month
in which to marry; it fell under the influence of spirits
adverse to happy households. Naturally no girl would
select unlucky May for her wedding. No, she waited
until May was past. But after May came June, so that
fortunate month fell heir to all of May's brides besides
having a full quota of its own. When Lent came into
being it represented a time of self-denial and sorrow;
but weddings are occasions of rejoicing. So the Lenten
season also tended to delay April and May marriages.

258

Why We Use A Wedding Ring

No wonder June became the bride's month, even among Christians.

The first Christians had been born Jews, inheriting Jewish customs; and in ages past Israelites decked their brides with a gilt coronet. This custom underwent slight changes, as have so many others, and our brides still wear the old Jewish coronet, though it now takes the form of a wreath of orange blossoms.

As everyone who has visited Florida or California knows, the branches of orange trees bear at the same time flowers and buds and ripe fruit, and in the proper climate the limbs are never bare. The old Saracens saw in this a sign of fecundity, so they selected orange blossoms as the fit ornament for the bride. Richard the Lion-hearted and his doughty Crusaders became familiar with the pretty conceit and brought it back to Europe with them.

The bride's veil is but the present-day development of the large yellow *flammeum* with which Greek and Roman brides were covered during the marriage ceremony.

See now what a strange blending of racial customs takes place during a wedding. The bride marches down the aisle of a Gothic cathedral to the German music of "Lohengrin"; she wears a Jewish coronet made of Pagan blossoms topping a Greek veil; on her finger she bears a Roman ring, not greatly dissimilar to that which marked the majesty of a king of Babylon; she

259

Why We Do It

kneels as did the brides of ancient Egypt in their temples and she contracts away her future in a ritual almost purely Anglo-Saxon. She speaks English until her first baby comes and then, "Ooky dooky dooky," she goes back to the murmuring prattle of Mother Eve.

And we men claim to understand them!

WHY WE HAVE AN ALPHABET

A CROSS Lake Titicaca, in Peru, the sun was setting six hundred years ago. From one of a small
cluster of huts, made of mud-plastered reeds, came an
old, old man, his red-brown skin wrinkled like a dried
apricot into marvelously deep ridges that ran in every
conceivable direction. He had no trace of beard, though
his long scalp-locks had been gray for many a year.
Around his loins he wore a band of gay-striped woolen
cloth, woven of the hair of the llama, that curious
creature with the body of a four-foot goat and the
upright long neck rising like a tree-trunk from its
shoulders. Because the evening air was chilly, even to
the old mountaineer, he had thrown across his back a
blanket of the same warm material, brilliantly dyed
in red, and blue, and purple, and yellow-orange. Aid-
ing his tottering legs with a stick held in the right
hand, the ancient Peruvian made pitiably weak haste
to another hut on the shore, before which sat a man,
similarly clad, smoking a tobacco-wrapped cigarette
while he gazed idly across the lake at the rose-colored
clouds in the west.

The old man arrived breathless from the exertion

of hurrying over the fifty yards which separated the two homes. The seated one looked up at him questioningly, but without speaking. Soon his visitor found breath, extending in entreaty a trembling hand from which dangled three or four colored strands of cord made from the twisted fiber of the *pita*. "Come," he gasped painfully, "you must get word to my son in Cuzco at the court of the Inca. He is to come at once. His mother is dying. He must come before two more suns have set if he would see her alive. Make haste, my friend, make haste, before Quipac comes by here on his way toward the capital. Make haste."

He dropped the strings into the outstretched palm of his neighbor. Then, his bleary eyes watering from excitement and the weakness of age, he watched the proceeding which had never—in his whole sixty-nine years—lost any of its fascination. His friend took the strands in a practiced hand, rapidly tying knots in a strange succession of sizes and shapes. To the old man this was incomprehensible; yet each knot had a definite meaning of its own which the scribes of Cuzco, forty miles away, would be able to decipher and understand. So quickly was it done that the caller's breath was still coming short and labored when the figure on the sand handed back the twine. "Here is your *quipu*," he said, relinquishing his cigarette; "Quipac will not pass here before half the sun is hidden in the lake. Your son will come."

262

Why We Have An Alphabet

The prediction proved true. Quipac, one of the Inca's corps of post-runners, passed this spot daily in his shuttling from Zapote to another government station eleven miles farther north; he carried official dispatches, received at Zapote and turned over to another messenger at the end of Quipac's route. Though it was against the law for the couriers to carry private messages, Quipac was a nephew of the old man. He slipped the knotted string into his pouch, handing it at the northern station to his relay, who delivered it to the son at Cuzco. A court chronicler read it, and before sun-up the second morning the son was at his mother's bedside, yielding her a last embrace.

When next you visit the Metropolitan Museum of Art in New York you will see, still preserved, several kinds of *quipus*, recovered from Peru, but absolutely undecipherable to the modern scientist. Yet this knot-system of writing was astonishingly complete. Statistics of crops, of gold production and other records were kept by this means; it was the only approach to writing that these people had ever discovered.

So we see that an alphabet is not absolutely essential for conveying thoughts from one mind to another far distant in time or space. Then how did we come to have that set of sound-symbols which we call our alphabet, and why?

Our American Indians give us a hint. Treaties still in existence, made between certain tribes and our Gov-

ernment, contain their text in two forms—English, for
our understanding; and in pictures, for the red men.
Similar pictures graven on a rock near Lake Superior
relate a bit of Indian history, recounting how and
where some of their number enjoyed an adventure on
a neighboring body of water. A wavy oblong outline
indicates a lake; on it float three canoes, each containing four men. A turtle reveals that they were of the
Turtle clan, while other marks disclose that they
caught five small fish and one of enormous size; a circle
near the water, with straight lines radiating only from
its upper arc, inform us that this took place about
five in the afternoon.

That was a good way to explain canoes, or other
concrete objects—as men or fish. But now suppose that
this Indian annalist had wanted to inscribe something abstract, like Shakespeare's phrase, "Let good
digestion wait on appetite." How would he go about
drawing "let," or "good digestion," or "wait on," or
"appetite"?

From the Chinese we learn how picture-writing was
enabled to set forth such undrawable thoughts. Thus
they had a circle to represent the sun, and a crescent
for the moon; by combining these they represented the
conspicuous common attribute of both luminaries—
"brightness"; "field" and "strength" united meant
"male"; the sun seen through trees, "the east"; because
of the crowded living quarters a pig under a roof sig-

nified "home." In this, of course, economy would suggest that when two pictures were required to bring out one idea the interfering and needless parts should be eliminated, only the essential lines and curves remaining.

That is how it happens that our learned men are quite unable to recognize the origin of many Egyptian hieroglyphs; for nearly all writing started as pictures, though the conservative Chinese still retain their primitive signs almost unchanged while the Egyptians quickly adopted abbreviated forms. Our own writing, and the marks with which we express sounds, came to us by devious routes from Egypt, China not having been "discovered" by white men until our civilization was well under way.

Egypt, being a prosperous and influential nation, was of course visited by those insatiable traders and merchants, the Phœnicians. These people were not particularly inventors, but they excelled in copying and adapting whatever of value they encountered in their far-reaching voyages to distant lands. They shipped cedar from Lebanon to Cairo, exchanging it there for pottery, jewelry, armor, clothing. With this cargo they sailed to the British Isles, taking on a load of tin in exchange; back again to Egypt where the tin was sold to the army quartermaster to be cast into bronze; and in return they were paid in gold with which they set sail for Phœnicia and home.

Why We Do It

We can imagine one of these shipmasters before a voyage being approached by a friend who would say, "Chaim, next time you go to Egypt I want you to take along a hundred fine sheepskins and sell them for me; I'll pay you a commission, of course." And Chaim, shrewd business man, would reply, "Sure, Yitzhok. Glad to accommodate; but the pirates are mighty plentiful this season; it'll be at your risk, you know, and the commission will have to be one-fifth of whatever I get. Got any reliable friends who want to do a little exporting? You know me."

That would require bookkeeping, so the wily Phœnicians learned from the priests and scribes of Egypt how to write. A man might perhaps wisely spend hours in drawing the hieroglyphs to be chiseled on a monument or painted into a state record; but for keeping personal accounts this delicate care would be needless. The quickest way would be the best way. Abbreviations of all sorts would be devised; and instead of writing each sound-sign separately the tendency would be to run them together to avoid the time-loss involved in lifting the pen or brush. In such manner did "cursive" script come into the world.

On settlement day there would be disputes, of course. Simonides, a merchant of Athens, would swear by all the gods on Olympus that he had entrusted to Chaim eighty-five metal shields for sale in Iberia. To which Chaim would retort scornfully, "How do you get that way? It's been a year ago now and you don't remember. I've got it written in my book here. I put it down at the time. Sixty-five it was—not eighty-five. Always it's the same old story with you. I notice you never remember that you gave me *less* than my manifest calls for—it's always more. How can you run a business like that? Get somebody to keep books for you. Or do it yourself. Here, I'll show you how. It's a pipe."

Thus came writing into Europe. The Greeks, being fond of literature, preserved their poems and stories in script; years later the Roman smart set journeyed to Athens to finish its education, absorbing Greek methods during the process. Can't you just see a Roman youth of twenty, his budding mustache just beginning to show a dark smudge across his upper lip, lording it over his associates back home? "Oh, yes," he would say, "you fellers should have seen that Olympic meet, especially the boxing. Gee whiz, that last bout, when Tunnicus whipped Dempsicus, was one pip, kiddo. Boy! Some cestus-work!! I've got it written down here by rounds and I'll read it to you. Now, what did I do with that papyrus? I remember I had— oh, yes, here it is. Round one—Tunnicus leads with his lef—what? These marks? Why, don't you know? Aw, don't tell me you don't recognize writing! It's just as easy! But of course you fellers have stuck around this stuffy old town all the time. Well, I'll tell you. There's a list of little ding-bats, each one different, and every one has a different sound. The first is called alpha and it sounds like 'ah'; the second is beta, like this—'buh, buh!' Alpha-beta, alpha-beta— of course, there's lots more of them than just these two, but because they come first we Alpha Sigma Sigmas in Greece used to call the whole bunch the alpha-beta—for short, you know." And so on, even more tirelessly and tiresomely.

The names by which the Greeks called the letters had been taken over from the traders of Sidon with the symbols themselves. The Phœnician called his first two letters "aleph" and "beth." The Greek found it easier to pronounce these as "alpha" and "beta," changing the shape of the marks a bit just as he did with their names. As nation by nation adopted the newly-imported art the letters grew more simplified in form, and standardized. There grew up a few aberrants —the Russians use a letter-form which appears quite strange to our eyes, as do the Persians and a few others. But in the main the white civilization uses one type of letter—we find it among the Italians, the French, the Germans, the Spaniards, the Dutch, the Norwegians and Swedes.

It was these Norwegians and Swedes who first employed letters in a manner which still exists among ourselves. To use strange quirks for preserving sounds struck these people as a deep and awesome mystery, savoring of magic; and because they used a magic

268

ritual over their dead they began to chisel literary sentiments on the stones that headed the grave. The marks, or letters, were known as runes. Runic inscriptions spread into Denmark, and then into the remainder of Europe, from whence we inherit the custom of incising epitaphs on the stone grave-monuments in our cemeteries.

Because our ancestors adopted the Egyptian glyphs they encountered one difficulty of which we have not yet rid ourselves. The Egyptians, of course, evolved their alphabet, or its equivalent, to represent the sounds that they used in their own speech. The Phœnicians, however, vocalized quite differently; so they twisted the borrowed signs to make them serve for several purposes. The Greeks did likewise. And—skipping the interval—we find ourselves doing the self-same thing. Thus you and I have to use one single letter— the *a*—to stand for such diverse sounds as we encounter in the words *a*ll, sen*a*te, *a*m, *a*rm, fin*a*l. Again, we have several ways of representing the same utterance— hysteri*cs*, ki*cks*, py*x*. Note that not only is the x-sound indicated in three ways, but the *i* and *y* are interchangeable. So we work some of our letters, like *a*, overtime while we give others one or more assistants.

Yet we are fortunate that our script descended from the Egyptian picture-writing. That has enabled us to reduce the sounds to 26 symbols. Think of trying to memorize more than 1,000, as we'd be compelled to do if our system had come from the Chinese! Nevertheless, the Chinaman, after he has learned that mass of graphs, writes with comparative fluency. But the ogam alphabet, used in Britain and Ireland about 500 A. D., though simple enough to learn is so slow in use that we should never have gotten on with it. The letters in ogam are indicated by short dashes reaching down to, or up to, or right through a horizontal line. When Ian Padhraic MacCarthy in Cork wanted to write to his lady-love in London he started the letter about like this:

(D E A R   S W E E T H E A R T)

After all, then, our alphabet, with its many duplications and shortcomings, isn't so bad, is it?

WHY WE KISS

THE ardent young wooer was trembling with exaltation in the presence of his beloved. Rapturously he gazed into her eyes, and his soul gushed forth in ecstatic bliss. Timorously, fearful of the outcome, he made question, "Will you b-be my w-wife?"

Coy and flustered, the maiden answered, "Yes."

Instantly the youth was transported to the seventh heaven of delight. His greatest wish in life was about to be fulfilled. Then, with the characteristic boldness of the male, he sought concrete evidence of the maiden's affection. His whole pulsing body demanded the chaste touch of salutation which is the lover's right.

So he leaned over towards the face of his darling and whispered, "Then, sweetest of women, most beautiful of all who have ever lived, may I—may I—may I rub my nose against yours?"

For they were Eskimos, you see.

To us the kiss is so natural an action that it seems instinctive, an inborn desire common to all people. But this is not the case. In fact, one-half of the world is entirely ignorant of it, except where kissing has been introduced by foreigners. Thus the Polynesians, the

271

Malays, the Burmese and other Indo-Chinese, the
Mongols, the Laplanders, the Eskimos, besides other
races (chiefly Asiatic) salute their intimates or relatives by putting noses together for the purpose of
sniffing or smelling.

How strange this custom appears to us! Yet is it
really more curious than the corresponding European
habit of salutation by tasting? In the Etymological
Dictionary Mr. Skeat connects the Teutonic *kussa,*
German *Kuss,* with the Latin *gustus,* taste. And while
in pressing our lips against people we have no actual
desire to get a sample of their flavor, so too the other
half of the world probably sniffs not to gain an idea
of odor but—as we do—goes through certain accepted
gestures as a sign of greeting, love or respect.

Evolutionists would perhaps explain these customs
as survivals from the time when man was still half
animal and greeted strangers, as dogs do now, by
mutual sniffing beginning nose to nose; and the kiss
might be considered a remnant of the affectionate licking which dogs and cats and other animals bestow
upon their cherished young, the habit having been
extended to include adults for whom was felt a strong
liking. But the Fundamentalist can point to different
greetings, prevalent in wide areas over the earth's surface, in which neither the nose nor the mouth take
part.

Thus the Andaman Islanders when meeting clasp

one another in their arms. The Australian blacks embrace under circumstances which would provoke a kiss of greeting among Frenchmen. On the other side of the world, in the bleak and chilly wastes of Tierra del Fuego, at the southern point of South America, the natives in friendly salute take pride in hugging each other with "the grip of a bear." And when we turn to other lands, under a state of far greater civilization, we find recorded similar methods of salutation. Genesis xxxiii, 4, tells us that "Esau ran to meet Jacob and embraced him"; in like manner Homer's Odyssey relates of ancient Grecian heroes that when Odysseus made himself known to them after a long absence Philœtius and Eumeaus cast their arms around him. Furthermore, among still other tribes, the usual form of salutation takes the form of patting, or stroking, or other caresses.

Those of us who have friends among Latin races are familiar with a rather remarkable performance of theirs employed when intimates meet again after a long absence or on the return from a journey. The two men will approach each other with widely extended arms; each will lay his head over the left shoulder of his friend while the arms of both clasp breast to breast in warm embrace. Then, releasing momentarily, they will move their heads to the right shoulder, repeating the hug; and each will pat the back of the other. After which ceremony they will shake hands.

273

Why We Do It

In contrast with this elaborate greeting is the simple salute of certain African tribes—savages, of course— among whom the accepted mode is to press the thumbs together. And among our own American red-skinned natives I myself have been welcomed by the customary raising of the right hand to the level of the head, the opened palm being turned forward—not greatly different, indeed, from the military salute rigidly enforced in the armies of the leading civilized nations.

As a matter of fact, the military salute probably sprang from the same source.

And here we arrive at the basic distinction between the two forms of salute. When the greeting is between equals, or at least between those who hold for one another a deep affection, the many instances cited show that in all corners of the world mankind exhibits a universal yearning to touch or to fondle as a token of welcome. However, as between two people whose positions are recognized by both as those of superior and inferior—as an army officer and a private, or a Congo husband to whom his wives kneel on his return from a prolonged absence—there is no contact of bodies, but merely motion or speech of some sort by each in recognition of the presence of the other.

This is quite understandable. Each of us feels a satisfaction in touching or caressing those for whom we entertain a lively affection. A mother never tires of pressing to herself or of petting and otherwise fondling

274

her adored infant. In less gentle but no less tender manner fathers display the same instinct, and a bit of observation will make clear how uniformly a word of paternal praise is accompanied by a pat, or a stroking of the head of the loved son or daughter. So, also, there is a similar though a weaker gratification in touching others not closely related but for whom we strongly care.

But towards those of the same sex whom we believe to be our inferiors we feel a revulsion which may be strong or mild. No pleasure would come to us from physical contact; that might even be quite distasteful. Hence our salutation is made at a distance. But this is not akin to the reverence which we harbor towards the powerful, or the great, or other superiors, although in this case also we salute from a distance to avoid the appearance of undue familiarity.

Have you noticed, though, that we have strayed somewhat from our subject? The question before us is, "Why do we kiss?" Fortunately it is a query which demands no lengthy exposition. Any man who has met one of the opposite sex who aroused his intense and admiring devotion knows without being told. Or, if he doesn't, a long, prosy account of the pleasure so secured would be of no value to him whatsoever.

Besides, he doesn't deserve it.

And as for the ladies—well, have you ever met one who would acknowledge that she derived any joy from the practice? Therefore it would be quite useless to explain.

Nevertheless, for the benefit of prospective experimenters, one might suggest that the rubbing of noses can well be left to the Eskimos.

WHY WE LIKE THE THEATER

IN the group was Mr. Samson Raphaelson, gifted young playwright of "The Jazz Singer." He had stopped in for a few moments on his way to the show-house for a rehearsal of his latest philosophic comedy, "Young Love." Of course the talk turned to shop. It always does. Somebody raised the question why people go to see a theatrical performance.

Freddie chipped in his say. "For amusement," he suggested. "Everybody likes to see a good show. There's entertainment, diversion, sometimes fun."

A writer offered a different version. "Seeing a play gives us a pleasant cross-section of life. No, that isn't it, either—people go to see an unpleasant show, one with a disagreeable ending—when they know in advance that the ending isn't happy. Maybe it's because they want to be released for a few hours from thinking and from the harsh realities of existence. Yes, that's it. They want release. It's like getting drunk in a refined way, and without the headache."

One turned to Mr. Raphaelson. "Sam, you're a playwright—why do people go to see a show?"

Raphaelson lit his pipe, carefully waved out the

277

flame, disposed of the match well out of sight, and countered with, "Why do people read books?"

"I asked you to answer a question, not to propound one."

"Ugh! Well, as I see it, humankind is distinguished from the animals by at least two traits that are important to us right now—the ability to laugh and the appreciation of form. Lovers of dogs claim perhaps that they have seen their pets express what we might call a grin. But I'm speaking of laughter—uncontrolled vocal sounds produced by the spasmodic action of the diaphragm plus the diverse physical postures necessary to—oh, hell, you know what I mean—just the forgetting of everything else in a loud fit of obvious gayety—throwing back the head and laughing. Men do that—all kinds of men, everywhere. No member of the brute creation does. So laughter is one of man's distinguishing marks, for the purposes of this discussion.

"And man likes to laugh. Don't forget that. Why, even sober, serious business men, who would resent any intrusion or interruption of their busy routine, voluntarily try to remember funny stories so that they can tell these to other business men while they're all closeted privately 'in conference.'

"And then—more important—there's the sense of form. It's hard to define that exactly. We see it in our fine paintings. The composition, the way the different objects and colors are disposed, and balanced, is an expression of form. Cut out those very objects, give them to an inferior painter, and he would put them together in another arrangement—a different form— and the effect would not be as good.

"We have form in music. One composer works up his materials to produce a great emotional effect—the wedding march from Lohengrin, for example. Yet you and I have at our disposal the very same notes that Wagner used in that masterpiece. Can you and I sit at our piano and create such a triumph? No. We can produce, at will, the selfsame notes, mind you. But you and I haven't the power to put them together in a new way and gain the same effect as Wagner did. We can't create that vast emotional upheaval in the mind of the listener. Why? Because you and I don't know how to put the notes together properly to secure that effect. We haven't Wagner's sense of form.

"All right. Now, every play—every good play, I mean—is essentially form. The writer visions certain characters, he senses certain situations between his characters, he determines the kind of effect that he wants these characters and situations to produce on the audience. Then he puts these and his other materials together—but, mark you, in a certain way, following a definite pattern of his own. That way of putting them together, that pattern, is the form of the play. If the form is right the author is far on his

279

way to producing a good play that people will enjoy seeing.

"So, to answer your question specifically, people go to see plays because actual life is formless; mankind craves form; therefore we go to plays to see plausible incidents from ostensible real life arranged into an interesting form. Put it another way: Life, as we live it, is not ideal. We recognize that. But we hope for the ideal. Well, in a good play we see life in ideal form— and we enjoy satisfying our natural craving.

"I said life is formless. If you want an example, take the life of one man. Say he encounters a problem one evening—he wants to marry the girl, but the girl's father objects. What does that man do? He walks away despondent, takes the street-car to the corner nearest his home, gets off, stops in at the cigar store for a pack of cigarettes, meets a friend who tells him a long and pointless story of business injustice, goes to his room, takes the newspaper out of his pocket, starts reading about last night's fight results—and so on. There's a whole string of unrelated and irrelevant incidents. It may be a week, possibly a month, before that man works out what plan he is going to follow; and meanwhile a thousand or ten thousand things can be happening, in all of which he takes a greater or smaller part. But those things are in no way related to the problem that we started with—love for the girl and her father's opposition. So life, as it flows along, is

280

chaotic, confused, jumbled—formless, as I said. But in
writing a play about that problem we'd skip all those
needless details, and we'd crowd into a tense two hours
of action and speech one pertinent incident after another, each building in logical sequence to the succeeding incident, all building up towards the final
master-incident—the climax. In that way we'd attain
form. That's what people pay to see."

Well! There was something to digest. But somebody
—there's always one like that in every crowd—somebody spoke up and said, "Yes, that's true of the drama,
no doubt. And, as a consequence, it's true of moving
pictures, for they are only dramas made in light and
shadow. But how about vaudeville? That's all split up
into twelve- and fifteen-minute turns. Where's any
form in that? But if you think people don't like to
see vaudeville, you try to buy seats for tonight at ——"

"Of course there's form in vaudeville," interrupted
Raphaelson. "Sure there's form in vaudeville. I'm glad
you mentioned that——" and then I knew that the
questioner was going to be pulverized. Whenever a man
who is expounding a theory says he's glad you brought
up a particular argument it's because you have put
your foot in his trap. And he knows it.

"See here," continued Raphaelson, "every one of
these separate acts has form. It starts in a given way,
develops in a given way, works up to its climax and
ends at just the right moment and in the right way.

281

Why We Do It

The singer doesn't do her hardest and most intricate song first and then go on to something simpler. No, sir. She starts easily, simply. You almost say to yourself, 'Why, I could do that.' The next song is different in motif, in tempo, in execution. You applaud. Her third number is different again—form, you see—and works on your emotions more powerfully than did the others. When finally she leaves the stage she has you clapping your hands until the palms redden. She captured you. Yep, there's form in every act.

"But there's form in the arrangement of the various acts, too. The evening's entertainment doesn't start with the star, followed by a juggler, then by a dancing team, then by a news reel, then by a musical sketch. Nixy. Experience, imitation and individual genius have worked out for vaudeville programs a form which is sure-fire with the average audience. Certain kinds of acts, arranged in a certain definite order—form, you see. Yes, I'm glad you mentioned vaudeville. Has anybody else any questions he wants answered?"

I should say not!

This view of the playwright's is upheld by Dr. Schmalhausen in his remarkable volume, "Why We Misbehave." Of course, the learned author by no means implies that attending the theater is a form of misbehaving. But he does explain, though in a somewhat different connection, why we revel in the illusions of the stage. In Chapter III he says, "Litera-

282

ture (and this applies with equal validity to poetry, drama, music, art in general), from time immemorial, has been a spiritual soothing syrup, a balm, an anodyne, a fairy-tale, mere pretense and make-believe, bravely set against the stern realities which the cowardly mind of man could not endure.

"Cosmically, we may say that the world was too much for the mind of man and but one road of escape led promisingly from out of the wilderness of his consciousness of inferiority: the road leading to the gracious land of make-believe and sweet mythology."

Again, in Chapter II, Dr. Schmalhausen speaks of "—the realization of man's childish delight in make-believe which he refers to as idealism. Man does not find it easy to absorb reality. Reality represents disharmony, imperfection, evil. His infantile imagination creates a private universe in which harmony, perfection, good, rule as the holy trinity of the inner life. Pretense soothes the mind of man, reality disturbs it."

Probably one explanation supplements the other. Raphaelson maintains that we enjoy the theater because we have a sense of form. Schmalhausen explains how our feeling for form originated. So the next time that you are at a show, convulsed with laughter, or eager, strained, intense at the drama unfolding before you, you may, if you wish, stop and say to yourself, "I am enjoying this because I have a sense of form, and I have a sense of form because my grandfather was a

283

sap." I say you may do this, if you wish. But you won't. And you are quite right. After all, how many philosophers have achieved happiness?

I don't know whether Wallace Beery has a sense of form, but I can laugh my head off over his pictures. It is probably best for the majority of us to remain sappy and happy.

WHY WE HAVE FORKS

IT is a gay but reverent company that is gathered at
the London inn this year of our Lord, 1609. Gay
because most of the feasters are young bucks of quality, privileged members of the royal court; reverent
because there sits at the head of the table Prince
Henry, eldest son of James I. They are congregated
to do honor to a returned traveler, a peculiar character with skill enough to be an author, audacity
enough to have become a sort of court fool, firmness
enough to follow his own ideas even when these run
contrary to accepted custom. This is Thomas Coryate,
a general favorite despite his eccentricities.

The talk is running high. Coryate is relating his
adventures, encountered during the previous twelve-
month in the course of a walking tour through France,
Italy and neighboring lands. The plumed and velveted
gallants in his audience contribute uninvited interrup-
tions in the forms of comments and questions, some of
a sort that are, to say the least, of questionable taste.
Yet each sally brings forth roars of laughter; waiting
only for the noise to die down, Coryate makes answer to
each speaker; and his daring innuendoes, his shrewd

285

parries against broad insinuations, his unashamed admissions of rapturous peccadilloes, excite the laughter to ever greater and greater heights. Truly, the guest of honor is in rare form tonight.

"So then I made tryst with the Roman damsel," continues Coryate. "Olive-brown was she of skin, her eyes large and black and melting——"

"Melting?" interjects a listener. "Melting? Then the bare sight of thee must have made her weep. Wert so distasteful to her?" An outburst of merriment rewards the neat thrust.

"Nay," retorts the suave Coryate, "they melted from the heat of my persuasion, so that her tears became vapor and her—— But here cometh mine host and his drawers, bearing brave burdens of victual and drink. Way for the viands! A cup of sack, most worthy host; mine throat is dryer than the Appian Way in mid-August."

So they fall to; the flow of chatter ended for the time being by the tempting meats set before them, except for an undertone of droning hum as each man mumbles to his neighbor. Then, suddenly, a silence falls. Each man in that noble company sits aghast, his lips parted in astonishment, as Thomas Coryate produces a pointed metal instrument, spears a bit of meat with it and conveys it to his mouth. The guests, after the first shock of surprise, gaze in consternation at Prince Henry. The royal scion speaks.

Why We Have Forks

"What hellish device is that, Coryate?" he demands.

"This, Highness?" inquires Coryate, holding the implement before him in simulated wonder at the question. "It is an forke, much in favor among the nobility of Italy. Its employment preventeth unseemly soiling of the fingers." And the intrepid innovator spears and eats another morsel.

Prince Henry gasps. "Preventeth unseemly soiling of the fingers? Unseemly soil—art thou then so ungrateful of the gifts of Providence that thou refusest to touch the wholesome food? Verily, it is an invention of the unbelievers!"

After this royal hint the company breaks into an uproar. Ridicule after ridicule is heaped on the head of the iconoclastic traveler. But he calmly eats through it all. "Ye will learn," he assures them with a smile. "Ye will learn. And ye will one day also each have his forke. Mark the prophecy."

The bold Coryate was right. The time came when every member of the royal family and of the court became possessed of a fork. Soon the previously universal habit of lifting all solid food to the mouth with the fingers fell out of use among the social leaders. Eating with a fork became the fashion. And, of course, shortly after the style had taken hold among the "Four Hundred" of that time, three centuries ago, it began to trickle down into the lesser nobility, the brewers, the merchants and thence into successively lower levels.

Why We Do It

Unlike lots of fashions this one had sense to it, so the use of the fork (Latin, *furca*) remained, though Coryate himself complained in one of his books that he was called "furcifer (fork-bearer)" by his contemptuous friends because he was the first among them to use "those Italian neatnesses, called forkes."

I can appreciate just how humiliated he may have felt about it, for to this day I simply cannot be sure when sitting down to a banquet whether it is the long or the short fork that one uses for pie, whether the broad flat one is for ice cream, salad or fish. I have tried waiting until somebody else starts, to follow his lead, but as often as not two people will use different forks when I'm around. Keeping an eye on the hostess is no good, because if she is tactful she will note an error committed by a guest and then she'll commit the same error so as to avoid embarrassing him—and folks would think that I was the one who made the mistake, not the other fellow. Once I schemed out a plan; I tucked all my forks away in my napkin in my lap, intending to reach down for one each time a course was changed; and since there'd be no other fork at my place everybody would be able to see that I had been compelled to use the fork that happened to be in my hand at the moment. But one of the servants noted the lack of tools and brought others to take their place, thus calling a fine quantity of undesired attention to me. Besides which, some officious idiot called on me for

288

a speech, and before I remembered I had risen to my feet. You could hear the falling forks clatter a mile and a half away, and it spoiled the speech—for me. No doubt the outraged hostess had the silverware counted twice that night. If she did it was a useless precaution. Why, the last thing in the world I'd steal would be an assortment of forks. What would I do with more than one? It would be like a sick man amusing himself by getting a complication of diseases.

Some people have a natural talent for the proper selection of table tools. Instinctively, it seems, they pick up the right fork at the right time, they know when to leave the spoon in the dish and when to lay it on the serving-plate underneath. But it's like spelling, I guess—if you're not born with the gift there's no use trying to acquire it. The best place to be invited is to a picnic.

Probably the earliest of eating tools was the knife— a flake of flint chipped to a fine edge. To be sure, it wasn't invented for that purpose. Primitive man had no idea of daintiness. What he sought was some method of dismembering his prey, and one day, perhaps, a wandering genius picked up a couple of flint stones by accident and began knocking them together in pure idleness. Bang! One of them flew apart in splinters. The experimenter picked up one of the chips and noticed that the edge was sharp. "Gosh ding it!" he exclaimed. "Here's just what I've been looking for.

289

Now when I snare a rabbit I can cut his legs off instead
of having to tear him apart. Darn good stunt!"
Naturally, the other members of the tribe would admire
that momentous improvement. They started out looking for flints to knock together. In some such manner
came into being the Palæolithic Age, the era of the
first stone implements, and with it the cutting edge—
the knife.

With shells of mussels and clams to be picked up on
the beaches and river banks it would seem unavoidable
that primitive man should have thought of using these
natural bowls for conveying food to the mouth. But
we must remember that early man probably had little
use for a spoon. His meat was first cooked by broiling
—he threw it into the fire or covered it with hot ashes
over a bed of glowing coals. Frying would occur when,
to avoid ashes in his food, he set a piece of fat meat
on a flat rock fixed in place over the flame. Boiling
was probably the last method of cookery discovered,
for, as a rule, there would be required pottery that
would remain uncracked while enduring heat on one
side and water on the other. Some tribes, it is true,
dropped hot stones into a skinful of water, but the
amount of liquid that could be thoroughly heated in
this way must have been rather small; and whether a
stew of wild meat could be prepared by this method
in time to suit the hungry hunter may be open to some
question.

Why We Have Forks

So, probably having no soups or gravies, and eating his berries and fruits as he found them, early man apparently had little need for a spoon. Nevertheless, the Greek word points to a shell as the ancestor of their spoons. Still, that word might conceivably have come into being long after spoons had been in common use, and when the shell with a stick fastened on for a handle had replaced the original form of spoon, just as the word stateroom is used by us to designate almost any of the bedchambers on a ship, though certainly such bedchambers were in use before there began the practice of naming them Wisconsin, New York, and so on, after the various states.

Color is lent to this view by the fact that our own word spoon is derived from the Old English *spon*, a chip or splinter of wood, comparable to the Dutch *spaan* and German *Spahn*, in the same sense; all these words very likely related to the Greek word meaning a wedge. And anyone who as a boy had to chop firewood knows that the splints cut from the main stem near a branch or fork commonly terminate in a dished or spooned-out place. It would be a simple matter to trim the edges of the hollow and to whittle the handle down to convenient shape, so forming a usable spoon. And fire-using men would encounter this phenomenon everywhere, while their trips to beaches or to the shores of large rivers where shell-fish might abound would be of rarer occurrence. So, by the law of chance, the

291

wooden spoon would appear to have a good claim as the forerunner of all other kinds.

Even in medieval times spoons were made of wood, and every housewife still has cooking spoons of the same material. Horn, too, because it can be bent into almost any shape when warmed over a fire, was a popular spoon-making substance in the olden days.

Along about the time when Columbus made his memorable voyage, spoons of brass and other cheap metals were in common use. But silver spoons were still a valued rarity, even royal households listing them in their inventories by careful individual description. Under date of 1259 an English will mentions the gift of a spoon to some heir of the deceased, in terms indicating that a high value was set on the article.

During the 15th and 16th centuries Apostle Spoons were all the rage. They were usually of silver, and the handle of each ended in a figure of one of the apostles. It was the custom to offer one of these as a baptismal gift, in which case the spoon bore the figure of the patron saint or name-saint of the child. There are still in existence complete sets of twelve, and even sets of thirteen, the spoon which bears the figure of Jesus being larger and more beautifully designed than the others.

A trace of this singular estimation of spoons has come down to us, as may be noted in the shops of almost any important resort visited by numbers of tourists.

Why We Have Forks

There will be found on display quantities of so-called "souvenir" spoons, having embossed on them some design emblematic of the spot. Souvenir spoons sold at Niagara show the Falls, as one example.

But how many times did you buy a "souvenir" knife and fork?

WHY WE WEAR JEWELRY

MAN is never satisfied with things as they are. In winter he makes artificial heat; in summer he creates cooling breezes with his electric fan. To many dry areas of the earth's surface he introduces water by means of irrigation and when it rains he raises an umbrella. In starting a village he selects an open space or chops down trees and vegetation to make a clearing, yet no sooner does the settlement grow into a city than he goes to huge expense to plant avenues of trees and decorate his yards with shrubs and other plants. As the astonished Frenchman remarked of the American and his mint julep, "He puts in whiskey to make it strong and water to make it weak; he puts in sugar to make it sweet and lemon to make it sour; he puts in peppermint to make it hot and ice to make it cold; then he says, 'Here's to you' and he drinks it himself. Poof!"

Yes, man's first concern with the world about him is to discover what is; and next he busies himself to change it about more to his own taste or liking. If the human race as a whole were compelled to adopt a motto, perhaps no more fitting one could be devised than, "Whatever is is wrong."

Man's dissatisfaction with things as they exist is by no means confined to outer objects. He considers himself the crown and summit of creation, but he isn't pleased with that, either. The most abject of savages almost invariably refer to their own tribe as "the men" or "the people," thereby delicately hinting that other tribes are to be classified as more or less akin to the beasts. And within the limits of this exalted and select group each individual rates himself as at least equal to any other member in point of physical attractiveness. You'd think that even man, self-centered egoist as he is, would be satisfied with that, wouldn't you? But no, to be the equal of the most tempting person of the world's most perfect tribe isn't enough for him. He has to improve on that, too. And leave it to him to know how to improve on the handiwork of his Creator! If God should ever make it known that He had committed an error in the construction of the universe there would be plenty of men immediately volunteering their advice on how to correct the deficiency. Mankind has lots of faults, but excessive modesty isn't one of them.

Consequently, among all tribes and in all ages, man has never hesitated to make himself more fascinating, or imposing, or gaudy. Previously in this book we have had occasion to discuss how he loves to paint himself

with vivid colors, and decorate himself with feathers
and glittering objects, and otherwise make an exhibi-
tion of himself by loading his body down with borrowed
brilliance. These practices are cheaply accomplished;
it costs no pain to stick plumes in the hair, or to smear
the skin with colored earths, or to string punctured
shells on a thong or fiber and hang it around the neck.
But even pain won't hold back man when he is bent on
adding to his ornamentation. He will endure the most
remarkable and agonizing mutilations, continued sometimes over months, to make his body approach closer
to his ideal of beauty.

Passing over such comparatively simple customs as
painting the eyelids black, coloring the nails yellow or
purple, dying the hair in various tints, staining the
teeth red, black or blue, we find that not one great
country can be named in which the aborigines do not
tattoo themselves. Tattooing is a long and painful
process during which coloring matter is forced under
the skin by means of a sharp-pointed instrument.
You'd think that such immolation would be about the
limit of human self-torture. Yet African tribes commonly cut long slits in their skin and then rub salt into
the wounds day after day so that, in healing, the scars
may stand out boldly—for beauty's sake. A traveler
relates that in Arab countries no beauty can be perfect until the cheeks or temples have been gashed.

The eyebrows and lashes are plucked out in some

parts of Africa and South America—and the custom
is not entirely unknown to our own ladies. In order
not to "resemble brutes," natives of the Upper Nile
knock out the four front teeth. Elsewhere, as in the
Malay Archipelago, the teeth are filed into points or
pierced with holes. The list could be continued, but our
present subject demands that we consider one special
kind of mutilation—perforation of parts of the face.

In both the Old and the New Worlds the upper or
the lower lip is pierced; in the hole is inserted a plug
of wood; and gradually, as the opening becomes
stretched, larger and larger discs of wood are inserted,
sometimes up to four inches in diameter—the size of
a small saucer!

Again, the nose is drilled, either through the septum
—the division between the nostrils—or the wings, for
the insertion of rings. And tribes all over the earth
pierce the ears; sometimes for the intrusion of wooden
discs which may from time to time be enlarged until
the ear's lower lobe touches the shoulder, sometimes for
the accommodation of rings of metal. This latter custom is prevalent among civilized women of today, and
in my youth I knew an Italian organ-grinder who wore
in his ears flashing rings of gold—a custom said by
authorities to be found still extant among the men of
many races.

The use of earrings dates from such remote antiquity that no one can say when it began. And in view

of what we have just read can we say with any pretence of justice that puncturing the ears for rings is right, while similar piercing for wooden discs in the nose or lips is wrong? If one such custom is justifiable, all are justifiable. If one is absurd, all are absurd. No?

Bracelets can boast an equally old and widespread sanction, having been in use among all known tribes and nations, savage, barbarian and civilized, from time immemorial. The paintings on the tombs of Egypt's long-buried kings show stalwart men wearing bracelets, of intricate design and made of precious metals, often so large as to cover the entire upper arm from shoulder to elbow. The ancient Medes and Persians, stern and pitiless warriors as they were, favored this sort of ornament for themselves. The Bible makes several mentions of bracelets, and in the Iliad we find evidence that the Greeks took great pains to adorn their arms with bracelets, among them being the spiral form which is recurrently popular even yet. Roman generals bestowed bracelets on their soldiers as rewards for acts of special bravery, and from the graves of ancient Teutonic heroes are taken bracelets along with their swords and shields.

In a former chapter we read of the practical uses of rings, and our own eyes give ample testimony to the rich elaboration lavished on those trinkets in our times. It has been so throughout the ages; as soon as the wearing of rings became permissible every aid that money could buy has been employed to make rings splendid.

Self-embellishment has not stopped here. The human love of finery has pounced on every available item of apparel that could be furbished up to make its wearer more gorgeous. A simple strap of leather will serve every purpose of a belt, but the leather has been gilded, and set with jewels, and even replaced by chains of richly chased silver and gold, heavily studded with gems; yet such weighty girdles must have been cumbersome in the extreme. Buckles, first devised for the utilitarian purpose of holding together parts of the clothing, have been so bedecked and bejeweled that they have evolved into the present-day brooches of lacy platinum and diamonds, costing in some instances more than a fine home for an average family. Buttons are made ornamental, from the bristling admiral's uniform to the serving-maid's cheap cape. Many a watch mechanism that won't keep time is encased in a costly cluster of jewels. Hatpins, six-shooters, shopping bags, saddles, filmy handkerchiefs, French heels studded with rhinestones, and cowboys' fancy-stitched boots, every article of apparel and personal use has been turned into an ornament for the human frame.

Westermarck, as quoted by Schmalhausen, writes, "There are peoples destitute of everything which we regard as necessaries of life, but there is no people so rude as not to take pleasure in ornaments. The ancient barbarians who inhabited the South of Europe at the time of the reindeer and the mammoth brought to their caves brilliant and ornamental objects. The women of the utterly wretched Veddahs in Ceylon decorate themselves in necklaces of brass beads. The Fuegians are content to be naked, but ambitious to be fine."

Yes, man has a passion for dolling himself up.

And, with it all, are we beautiful? Well, take a look at the portraits in the family album any time you want a good laugh.

INDEX

Names of authors from whose works important examples have been drawn are printed in CAPITALS.

A

Alexander the Great, 99, 254
Alphabet, 261.
Anger, 103.
Archimedes, 58.
Arnold, Benedict, 96.
Arrow, 53, 65, 67, 155.
Authors, 143.

B

Barber Poles, 78.
Bath, 60, 222.
Beards, 84, 85, 99, 100.
Beauty, male, 83, 84.
Beds, 206.
Belief, 164.
Best man, 19.
Bible, 195, 197, 298.
Black for mourning, 137.
Blush, 171.
Books, origin of, 195.
Bow and Arrow, 53, 65, 67, 155.
Bowing, 40, 42.
Bracelets, 298.
BREWER, 23.
Brides, 17.
BROWNE, 53, 139.
Burial, 32, 53, 54, 141.
Bush for wine, 80.
Button and Buttonhole, 132, 133, 134, 135, 136.

C

Candles, 141.
CHAMBERS, 56.

Chicle, 220.
Christ, 31, 32, 33, 93, 103, 113, 125, 141.
Clay writing, 195.
Coats, 65, 130.
Cohannim, 115.
Coiffure, 99, 101.
Collar, 132.
Commandments, 31.
Cooking, 218, 290.
Coronets, 259.
Cough, 200.
Credulity, 164, 168, 184.
Crouching as sign of submission, 41.
Crucifixion, 32, 126.
Cuneiform writing, 194.

D

DARWIN, 37, 38, 39, 42, 171, 296.
Dead, respect for, 141.
Decoration of self, 85 et seq., 100, 295 et seq., 299.
Demosthenes, 89, 90, 91.
Diamonds, 233, 299.
Drug-stores, 81.
Dwarf, 105.

E

Ear-rings, 297.
Eastman, George, 28.
Eating Habits, 107 et seq.
Edison, Thomas, 28, 252.
Egypt, 98, 99, 196, 209, 213.
Eskimos, 271.

301

Index

Index

Index